Help! My Teenager is an Alien

'Sarah Newton has written a beautiful book for working and living with teens. Take heed readers – your life is about to change for the better if you follow her lead! Thank you Sarah for writing this book for your readers and clients – I know they will benefit greatly.'

Diana Haskins, author of *Parent as Coach*

'*My Teen's an Alien* is such a breath of fresh air. Sarah's passionate, practical and honest approach to parenting your teen is contagious and will quickly have you seeing that YES there is light at the end of the tunnel.'

Gabriella Goddard, author of *Gulp! The seven-day crash course to master fear and break through any challenge*

'Sarah, congratulations on compiling all your hottest tips and techniques into one tidy package! Desperate parents asked – and you listened. Well done. Thanks to you, my son is no longer an alien – he is one of my closest friends. Prior to your bold, straightforward, no-nonsense coaching, I could barely stand to be in the same room with Ryan. Now, I can't wait for each moment with my son, who is

a 'Grade A' teen, just as he is. Two short years ago, we were BOTH behind bars (Ryan literally, me figuratively). Today we are free to be completely who we are with a lifetime of precious moments ahead. In my (humble) opinion, every wise parent will read your book and launch immediately into action – because this stuff really works! Those who choose not to will ultimately come back around once they exhaust all their other options with little success; so you do the math. Why wait?'

Chris Sfassie, creator of the Grade-Maker

'*Help! My Teenager is an Alien* is an easy-to-follow book about how to understand and help your teen throughout those troublesome years. I can honestly say, I now look forward to my daughters' teenage years knowing that with this book I've got the tools and understanding to create a happy environment in my home.'

Imke, mother of two

'Do you feel trapped by your children? If so, this is THE book to turn to. Aimed at parents of teenagers, Sarah's book will free you from those feelings! Her fresh and exciting approach supports, guides and challenges the reader. Using case studies and personal anecdotes she demonstrates the success of practical tools in action. Her insights shine a light onto deeper issues about oneself and onto the vital parent–child relationship that is developing. This is a gripping read that is both liberating and inspiring. I would recommend it highly to all parents, even to those with younger children.'

Clare Hanbury-Leu, director of Young Solutions
International and mother of two

'Help, my six year old is going to become an alien . . . or she was until I read this book. I don't know what made me read a book on Teens and Aliens but once done, could not put it down. You know that feeling you get when someone literally puts the solution on a plate for you, all you've got to do is pick it up and do something with it. Well, that is what Sarah does in this book; offers solutions and, with your commitment, ensures they work. I promise you, you won't be disappointed. You think this is for teenagers only. I tried the state and choice section with my six year old and have not looked back.'

Dan, father of two

'Parents, if your teenager is trouble then this is the book you need. Sarah is amazing and with her help you can reform your child. Buy it!'

Chrissie Venables, teacher and Head of Hall,
Hazeley School, Milton Keynes

'A year on from the TV series and the changes in my house are still amazing. Working with Sarah, my daughter experienced a 180-degree turnaround. My daughter is now a brilliant, fantastic, motivated teenager.'

Charlene, mother of Sairah, participant in
My Teen's a Nightmare, I'm Moving Out!

'I think you are one of the people that have helped me most and I think that you know teenagers sometimes better than they know themselves. I think you have some of the best ideas to help teens and parents cope and I think that you also use all this to make the teen and parent more confident with each other and in themselves. This book will help anyone who reads it and even though it is for parents, I will buy a copy for myself.'

Nicola, sixteen years old

'Before I met Sarah I was a nightmare! She helped me turn my life around and with this book you can turn your teenager's life around too.'

Melissa, participant in *My Teen's a Nightmare, I'm Moving Out!*

'Sarah has this amazing ability to connect with teens and help them find solutions that work for them. Sarah is like my daughter's favourite aunt who always has time to listen and has just the right words of support and guidance. Even though I am a very experienced coach, I am just too close to my daughters to give them the support they need at this time in their lives. Thank you Sarah for making a difference to the teen years in our house.'

Carolyn Matheson, Master Certified Coach

'Sarah is an inspiring coach. Sarah empowered, enabled and motivated me and I just love her humour! Through Sarah I was able to adjust my parenting which saved my relationship with my son. I moved into a more supportive role and absolutely believed in his ability to be the responsible young adult he has become.'

Margaret Hickman, parent

Help! My Teenager is an Alien

The Everyday Situation Guide for Parents

SARAH NEWTON

MICHAEL JOSEPH

Published by the Penguin Group
Penguin Books Ltd, 80 Strand, London WC2R ORL, England
Penguin Group (USA) Inc., 375 Hudson Street, New York, New York 10014, USA
Penguin Group (Canada), 90 Eglinton Avenue East, Suite 700, Toronto, Ontario, Canada M4P 2Y3
(a division of Pearson Penguin Canada Inc.)
Penguin Ireland, 25 St Stephen's Green, Dublin 2, Ireland (a division of Penguin Books Ltd)
Penguin Group (Australia), 250 Camberwell Road, Camberwell, Victoria 3124, Australia
(a division of Pearson Australia Group Pty Ltd)
Penguin Books India Pvt Ltd, 11 Community Centre, Panchsheel Park, New Delhi – 110 017, India
Penguin Group (NZ), 67 Apollo Drive, Rosedale, North Shore 0632, New Zealand
(a division of Pearson New Zealand Ltd)
Penguin Books (South Africa) (Pty) Ltd, 24 Sturdee Avenue, Rosebank, Johannesburg 2196, South Africa

Penguin Books Ltd, Registered Offices: 80 Strand, London WC2R ORL, England

www.penguin.com

First published 2007
1

Copyright © Sarah Newton, 2007
The moral right of the author has been asserted
All rights reserved

Definition of 'discipline' (p. 195) reproduced from 'Collins English Dictionary –
Concise Edition' with the permission of HarperCollins Publishers Ltd.
© HarperCollins Publishers Ltd 1982, 1988, 1992, 1995, 1999, 2001, 2006
(published as the Desktop Edition, © HarperCollins Publishers 2004)

Every effort has been made to trace copyright-holders and we apologize
in advance for any unintentional omission. We would be pleased to insert
the appropriate acknowledgement in any subsequent edition

Without limiting the rights under copyright
reserved above, no part of this publication may be
reproduced, stored in or introduced into a retrieval system,
or transmitted, in any form or by any means (electronic, mechanical,
photocopying, recording or otherwise), without the prior
written permission of both the copyright owner and
the above publisher of this book

Set in 12/17 pt Monotype Garamond
Typeset by Rowland Phototypesetting Ltd, Bury St Edmunds, Suffolk
Printed in Great Britain by Clays Ltd, St Ives plc

A CIP catalogue record for this book is available from the British Library

ISBN: 978-0-718-14971-0

This book is dedicated to my two teenagers in training, Bronte and Freya, who teach me so much about life and myself, to Eddie, my eternal teenager who makes everything worthwhile, and to all the thousands of teenagers who have made my journey possible. Thank you all.

Contents

Acknowledgements

I would like to thank:

Barbara and Douglas for all your hard work and dedication in supporting me with this book. Without you, this book would make no sense at all.

My Dad, who always made me believe that anything was possible, my Mum for sticking by me (even when she didn't agree) and my brother Craig, who always reminds me to keep my feet firmly on the ground.

Dan, Margaret and Carol for the long journey we have all been on together and for supporting me through my truly insane moments.

Diana Haskins for sharing the Parent as Coach philosophy with me and inspiring me to begin my journey.

Gabriella Goddard, author of *Gulp!* for never letting me lose sight of my goal and joining me for many 'afternoon teas'.

Debbie Catchpole from Fresh Partners for believing in me – who ever knew that the journey would be so long?

Kate and all the team at Penguin for taking on my wacky idea and making my dream a reality.

Terry and Julia, for all the enthusiasm you show for all I do, and all my friends for the late-night suppers of wine and tortilla chips that make it all worthwhile.

My long-suffering family, Eddie, Bronte and Freya, who helped me birth this alien, never lost hope and kept me going. I love you all.

And last but not least, all my amazing clients – without you this would never have been possible.

Our Supported Charity

Ten per cent of all our profits will be donated to The Red Balloon national charity.

Red Balloon specializes in the recovery of bullied children. These children have been so badly bullied that they are unable to go to mainstream school for fear of further humiliation, ostracism or threatening behaviour. Red Balloon offers a safe learning environment so that students can regain their self-confidence, get themselves back into a learning frame of mind and begin to succeed academically. Once these goals have been achieved we help students return to mainstream school, go on to college or begin their adult life in employment of their choice.

Red Balloon Learner Centres are for students between the ages of eleven and seventeen years, who have decided they can no longer go to mainstream school because they have been badly bullied. Often by the time they get to us they have been 'imprisoned' in their home because they are too frightened to go out. We have three aims at Red Balloon for you if you are one of these students. The first is to raise your self-esteem, the second is to get you back on an academic track and the third is to get you back into mainstream school, on to sixth form college or into employment.

Introduction – The emergence of the teenage alien and what we are going to do about it

It was all so easy in the beginning. There you were with a tiny bundle of joy. You cooed and looked at them with affection. It was all you could do to stop yourself from bursting into tears at the thought of your little darling. Then they took their first steps, spoke their first words and soon had their first day at school. That heartbreaking moment when you had to leave them all alone, they clung to your leg and begged you to stay and you felt like your evil twin as you walked away to the wails of, 'Mummy!' How much did you cry that day? The parents' evenings followed and they started growing out of shoes quicker than anything ... their first part in the school play ... their first award. Gosh! You were as proud as punch ... being a parent is the best thing in the world!

But Wait! What Happened?

One night they went to bed. All was well, you tucked them in, kissed them goodnight and talked about what you would do tomorrow, and in the morning ... Arrghh! Help! Your teenager has turned into an alien! You cannot even get them out of bed; suddenly your charming conversations have turned into a succession of grunts, slamming of doors and the over-use of words such as, 'Whatever!' They look the same as they did the day before but something has changed, something is different, something has taken over your child.

Never fear, help is here!

Together we are on a mission, a mission to turn your teenager back into a human being. I know how to speak their alien language and together, we can rid your teenager of the alien within!

Okay, on a serious note now, I know that living with a teenager is no joke. They can be irritating, irresponsible and downright disobedient. However, they can also be funny, lively, curious and adventurous, and having a great relationship with your teenager can be the most rewarding experience you can have. This book was born out of my love and passion for ensuring that parents can become influential in their teenagers' lives, that hitting the teenage years does not have to mean confusion and bewilderment. Teenagers can teach us so much about the joy of life, the joy of experiencing things for the first time, the joy of having your whole life ahead of you with so many things to do. Teenagers have their own set of rules, they are not 'blighted' by the social norms. They speak out on things they are passionate about, they throw caution to the wind, take risks and don't worry about how foolish they may be. Isn't there a lesson that we can all learn from that? There is no better feeling than seeing your child blossom into an independent young adult with their own mind, a child who will achieve great things and has learnt from you to be a great person. By reading this book I hope that every parent can share this experience.

Now, before you ask, I am not a parenting expert, nor do I choose to be – I just know a lot about teenagers. What does that mean? Well, what it means for you is that everything I talk about in this book comes from my experience of working with teenagers and their parents. It is from the mouths of the teenagers, their real words and what they tell me they want from their parents, and that is why it works. No science, no psychobabble and no degree needed. Hence you will get simple, no-nonsense steps in plain English. I will not be telling you what to do, I will simply be giving you information so you can choose what you want to do – after all, you are an adult! And it is no good telling me that your teenager is too bad or this will not work with them, because I simply will not believe you. I spent seven years working with young offenders, so there are not many situations you and your teenager are in that I have not seen before. Forget making excuses. Also, before you ask, this book is not about getting your teenagers to do what you want them to do, it is not about controlling them to be perfect teen-robots. **It is about understanding and appreciating the situations you and your teenagers are in so that you can make more empowering choices, which will ultimately lead to increased responsibility and independence and a less stressful home life.**

Understanding the Teenage Years

Before we start, I want to give you a little background so you can understand and begin to appreciate the situation you and your teenager are in. Most parents tell me that the emergence of the teenage alien is almost instant. One day they put their beloved to bed as a child, the next morning, the child who wakes up is a teenage alien. Why? To understand this change, let's take a brief look at child development:

0 to 6 years: Teacher Role

Think of the first six years of your parenting life as you being a teacher to your child, teaching them everything they need to know, to gain all the information for later life. This is the stage where your precious baby needs to learn everything from you, the adult in their lives. This is by far the stage most enjoyed by parents.

7 to 12 years: Manager Role

The next stage occurs between ages six and seven when a child moves from 'learning to read' to 'reading to learn', and as your child moves through this phase, you become a manager in their lives, the administrator so to speak, as they begin to initiate activities and become more social. Your child's social circle moves beyond just you and they turn to other sources to learn about life. These years are far less demanding of the parent and it is during this time that the parent is setting the stage for the teenage years to come. If you cannot handle the discussions about small tasks like washing up at this stage, then how on earth are you going to deal with the drugs and sex conversations in the years to come?

13 years onwards: Coaching Role

When your children approach thirteen, something even more extraordinary happens and their cognitive ability begins to develop. They start to realize that life exists outside their own world, and begin to experience emotions that they have never experienced before. They become unsure about themselves and their new level of thinking. The teenage alien begins to emerge as they try harder and harder to make sense of their new 'humanness'. They shut off from the outside world, choosing alien-type behaviour as a defence mechanism until they themselves find out what it is to be human.

During this stage, the parent needs to move with the teenager into a different communication style. Your teenager no longer requires you in your former role, you are now needed in a more supportive role. Try to manage and control your child and you will get nowhere. **As a parent you need to manage yourself first, so you, in turn, can be the support to your teenager.** Your teenagers no longer want you to manage them, they need you to coach them. As you have bought this book, my guess is that you are stuck in your old manager role, but the manager has been fired and you are no longer sure what your job is. As you try to manage more, your teenager moves further away from you. Let go of the manager

– it's time to move on. My job is to encourage you to grow with your teenager and for you to adopt more of a coaching role.

Have fun, your journey is just beginning.

Sarah – The Coach for Parents with Teenagers

When people find out what I do, it is normally met with an interested 'How did you get into that?' question. I do find it difficult to answer in one sentence. I have, after all, been training all my life to do this.

I was a really lucky kid. I came from a very stable home and my dad was not averse to the odd bit of Steven Covey material, so while most other children were watching TV, I was reading *Seven Habits of Highly Effective People*. I was immersed in self-development from a very early age and was always led to believe I could be and do anything I wanted. I truly thought that everyone had the same sort of upbringing.

The truth, however, was far more shocking and affected me deeply.

My dad, sick of the local kids hanging around, started a youth club when I was about nine. I thought it was so cool as I was able to hang out with the big kids. Every Friday night, there I was at the teenagers' disco and they all looked after me so well. They loved my dad and because of that they loved me too. I recognize now that he may have been the first person in these young people's lives to care about them. I particularly remember two young lads, Chris and Tom. I thought they were the bee's knees as they would sit and talk to me for hours, always making sure I was happy and even, on the odd occasion, sorting out people who were picking on me. They were the kindest, gentlest and funniest people I had ever met. I never remember feeling as alive as I did that summer.

I learnt very fast, though, that all was not as it seemed. I remember hearing whispered murmurings coming from the kitchen one night and my dad leaving in haste. However much I quizzed mum she would not tell me what had happened. I just knew something was wrong – I could feel it in the air. I waited up for dad for as long as I could but eventually fell asleep on the settee hoping that morning would bring the answers. Dad woke me early with a very serious look on his face. 'Sarah,' he said sternly, 'I need to talk to you about Chris and Tom.' It transpired that they had been arrested and, because of previous convictions, it was likely they would go to jail. I remember feeling devastated. I could not believe it; they were not criminals, they were my friends.

That day my life changed. I realized that people did not all get an equal chance, that some made decisions that were bad, not because they wanted to but because they did not know anything different. I sat in my bedroom and vowed that, because I did know something different, I would never ever be tempted to break the law, take a drug or do anything bad. I felt that I had to make the right choices for those that could not. From that day onward I have always refused drugs and I have never committed a crime. I really did, and still do, take the moral high ground because I did not want to let Chris and Tom down. So, many of the decisions in my life were moulded at the age of nine. Tom had always said that he wanted to go to America and work, so I decided I would go instead (and, sure enough, at twenty I worked at Disney for a year). I decided I would get married and have children late because Chris often complained about being a teenage father. I stuck to every promise I made to myself that night my summer was torn apart.

My teenage years were pretty uneventful. I was highly driven, highly motivated, challenging, principled and maybe slightly rebellious but I never did anything really bad – despite the long list of juvenile delinquents that I tried to save. I was a normal kid. I left school, went to college, went to Disney World to work and spent seven years of my life working in hotel and catering management (which was a posh word for pub manager). Chris and Tom were far from my mind. I did see them once when I went back home but the drugs had done their work and they were like empty shells.

I had almost forgotten my calling; my promise to save teenagers was far from my mind. Then it happened. I was watching TV and something about rent boys came on and all the feelings I had that day when I was nine came flooding back. I was strong – I had to help those who were not. On the spur of the moment I made a decision. I was going to be a police officer. Now, as you can imagine, most people discouraged me (especially my dad) but I was undeterred and after a year's selection process (this was the time when 10,000 people applied to the 'Met' for 1,000 places), I got in.

Now I do have to say the police and I were never a great fit. While I was busy trying to save the kids, I felt that the rest of the 'Met' were trying to lock them up. My entire probation felt as if I was fighting the system. After two years of dealing with young offenders like a conveyor belt, I just gave in and succumbed. Don't get me wrong, I did not forget my purpose, and the relationship that I had with most of the local youths was second to none. They told me things that perhaps they shouldn't have and that I was too nice to be a copper. I had no time, however, to save them ... that was until I met Luke.

Luke was funny, humorous, handsome and gregarious. He had bright skin and big blue eyes that always had a mischievous glint in them. He was also a persistent offender. It felt as if I spent more time with Luke than I did with my own family. His ins and outs to the police station spanned a two-year period. As time went on his eyes became grey and his skin sallow.

His humour seemed to pack its bag, his looks went down the drain and gregarious turned into downright annoying. It did not matter what I did, I could not stop him offending.

One day I led Luke from the police van to a prison cell. That was the last time I saw him because later he took his own life. Luke was disengaged, demotivated and apathetic about life. He had no adult to guide or support him. He felt a failure. I felt helpless and useless, unable to make a difference. I had failed again. I spent weeks not knowing what to do. I wondered if it really was possible to change things. Where had I gone wrong? What was I to do? I then remembered something that my dad used to say, 'Sarah, every-one has a gift; when we find it we have cracked it.' I realized that was what I needed to do; I needed to look for the gift in each young person I saw. So when young offenders came my way I began to ask different questions like, 'What drives you in life?', 'What is important to you?', 'What are you passionate about?' I started to look at them differently. I began to see young people in front of me who had purpose, drive, motivation and, of course, a special gift. I remember one boy who, in three months, turned himself around and began teaching other kids about the dangers of cocaine just by me asking him, 'What is the gift in this situation? What can you give to others?' I had finally found the key to unlock these young people from their patterns, perspectives and their miserable lives.

I spent the next nine years of my life after that moment getting through to young people who had previously seemed unreachable. My passion was eventually born into a business and, as I said, the rest is history.

When I see young people now, I really do see the gifts they have, the gifts they can give to others, the gift of hope they can give themselves. So the next time you are on the street and see a gang of teenagers, will you cross over? Will you ignore them? Will you check your bag whenever a teenager walks by? Will you believe everything you read in the press or will you be brave and look for the gift? Look for the gift and you will find it; look for the gift and you will see things in our young people that you have not seen before. **Look for the gift in your own teenager and you will be both surprised and pleased.** If you think they don't have a gift, look again, you're just not looking hard enough.

Sarah – The Parent

. . . not perfect, and proud of it!

When I meet people and they find out what I do, the first thing they say to me is, 'You must have perfect kids!' After reminding them there are no such things, I gently answer them with a firm 'No' and you know what, I am pleased I don't have perfect kids. Each day I learn something from my children. Each day I grow as they do and their imperfections are what I love the most – the way my nine-year-old gives me the most evil looks (she could put Medusa to shame) and the way my five-year-old folds her arms and stamps her feet with a loud 'It's not fair!' My kids are not perfect and neither am I, and for that I am greatly appreciative. Would you really want to be perfect every day? How boring!

So, after I say that resounding 'No' when people ask me if I have perfect kids I then say, 'But I am great at managing myself around them.'

I was never a natural parent. It was never something I dreamed of being; in fact, if I remember, it was the last thing I was ever going to be! So to say motherhood came easily to me could not have been any further from the truth. I remember looking at my daughter, Bronte, and wanting to scream – what on earth was I supposed to do with her? And then the advice comes, doesn't it? Do this, don't do that, do leave them crying, don't leave them crying. I watched other mothers as they cooed and wondered what was wrong with me, and why I didn't feel that way.

It was my dad who showed me the light in one erratic phone call. He just said to me, 'Sarah, you know she's not really a baby, she is just a small person!' Aha – now a small person I could deal with. So from that day forth my whole approach to being a parent changed. My job was clear – **it was my responsibility to raise a responsible and independent young adult** and that is what I was going to do. The first thing I did was write myself a 'Parenting Purpose' – a job description, so to speak. I asked myself questions such as, 'What do I believe?', 'What is important to me?', 'How do I want my children to be in the world?'

Here is what I wrote:

My purpose in parenting is to listen, understand, respect and empower. I am here to ensure my children learn, develop and grow into fine human beings who are responsible, compassionate and independent. I bring to parenting a lightness of spirit and a joy of life, and encourage this in my children. I ultimately believe that I can learn as much from them as they can from me.

My whole approach to my small person changed. While other mothers would stop their children crawling on the gravel because it hurt too much, I would let Bronte do it, knowing that she needed to make the mistake in order to learn from it. While other parents responded to one-word requests from their children, I demanded a sentence. Yes, others scowled at me and didn't agree with me but I didn't care. I knew, and still do, that I was doing, and am still doing, the right thing for me and my kids.

Now school was a different thing, as not only do you have the opinions of other parents but the teachers as well. But I stood firm in my beliefs. Like the day Bronte wouldn't get dressed. I told her she had five minutes and we were going whether she was dressed or not. She wasn't and we went (I took a school bag of her clothes with me and she got changed in the toilets after I told the teacher what had happened). Harsh as it may have been, since then, at 7.30am every school morning, without fail she is dressed and down-stairs and she knows that she is responsible for getting dressed at the correct time.

Then there was the time when we got in the car and she had left her homework inside and we left without it. My daughter now knows that she is responsible for making sure her homework is done and in her bag.

The other morning I was in the playground and a few parents were talking about how they were telling their children that they had to play with all the girls to be fair. They asked me what I did and I said, 'I let my daughter make her own choices – after all, I won't be there when she's older.' It was at that moment it struck me that most of the decisions we make as parents are not based on what we want or even what our child wants; they are based on us not losing face and on what other people will think of us. When I tell the pyjama story to other parents they say, 'Oh, I could never do that. What would people say? I would be too embarrassed.' I say, 'Who cares? This is your child and it is your job to ensure he or she becomes responsible and independent. If you cannot teach them things now, then what hope do you have for later?'

When my second daughter, Freya, was born things were so much different. She was, and still is, referred to as the small person – shortened to 'Smalls' or 'Person Four'. That is what she is – the fourth person in our family. She has as much right as the rest of us and as much say. At five she regularly tells us off and enforces house rules. Family decisions (but not financial ones) are made at the table with each of us having an equal vote.

So there I am, as a parent, not perfect, and proud of it – just doing my job! It reminds me of the famous words from Kahlil Gibran:

Your children are not your children. They are the sons and daughters of Life's longing for itself. They come through you but not from you, and though they are with you, yet they belong not to you.

They are not really mine. My job is to train them for life. A totally enjoyable and varied life, full of ups and downs like cutting yourself on gravel and going to school in your pyjamas!

1

My teenager has no respect for me and will not do anything I say

In fact, if I get a grunt these days I am lucky.

In this chapter we shall deal with the problem of gaining respect from your child. You may be interested to learn that this is the issue that I am asked for help with the most. So, it would be fair to say that you are not alone and you are certainly not the first parent who has faced this challenge.

I am a great believer that to gain respect we must first give it. We then have to show teenagers how to give respect. So, in this case study you will see how that was done.

We will follow Lyn and John's journey as they help their son to become a respectful human being.

Case Study: Lyn, John and Alan

....

Lyn and John came to me regarding their son Alan. Alan was seventeen years old and would not do anything his mum said. He was really rude, he had lashed out at her a few times and he almost ran the house. He often spent all day in bed and expected his mum to do everything for him, ordering her around as if he was in a hotel. When his mum and dad tried to speak to him they would just get grunts or swearing. They were frustrated and felt he was completely taking advantage of them. John was an executive in a large company: his work was demanding and kept him away from home, often leaving Lyn alone to deal with Alan. They were at their wits' end and were very close to asking him to leave, despite how much pain it would cause them.

When I am dealing with a parent who is faced with these challenges, I never underestimate how exasperated they are by the whole situation. Feeling that your child has no respect for you after all that you have done for him is devastating. 'He doesn't respect me' – a phrase we use so often and yet do we really think about what we are actually saying? When I take on a parent who comes to me with this issue, the first things I ask them are very simple: 'What do you want?' and 'What are the outcomes you want to see?' While on the surface these questions seem very simple, really they are not. When I asked Lyn, all she would say was, 'I want him to respect me.' As I delved deeper I asked her, 'What would that look like? How would you know you were being respected?' Her answer remained the same . . . 'He would respect me.'

Here was Lyn's first point of learning. She had given control to her son and was not taking any herself. By saying, 'I want him to respect me,' she was almost resigned to the fact that there was nothing she could do and she had to wait for him to do something first. No wonder she felt exhausted; she wanted her own life to change by waiting for someone else to make the first move. As I was coaching her and not Alan, there was no way I could make Alan do anything. In the same way, I cannot make your teenager do anything when I am speaking to you. Lyn had given up her power and was allowing Alan to be in charge of how she felt every day.

TIME OUT

Remember, the only person you can control is yourself. We cannot necessarily make anyone else do anything. When we think we can control another person we really are giving away our power to them by assuming our destiny is in their hands.

'What makes you think I can make Alan respect you when I am not coaching him?' I asked. After a few moments of silence she said, 'Well, I know you can't change him.' 'Can you change him, Lyn?' I asked . . . yet again silence, followed by a very quiet, 'Well, no.' 'Who are you in charge of, Lyn?' I asked, venturing into what felt like uncharted water. 'Only me,' she said. I could almost feel her shoulders drop, the pressure had been lifted. Lyn had realized that she no longer had to worry about 'changing' Alan. She had to be more in charge of herself. Her first week's homework was to look at where she gave up her power/control to Alan and what triggered her to do this. I wanted her to understand where she felt most powerful and in control and how she could use that in her relationship with Alan.

Lyn went away and compared her work situation to her relationship at home with Alan. She found that at work she felt totally powerful and in control. She never blamed anyone else for her feelings or when things went wrong. She took 100 per cent responsibility for herself. If she had a problem with a colleague, she never went around saying, 'He doesn't respect me, make him respect me.'

I asked Lyn what was different between work and home. She agreed that on the surface nothing was different, but when she dug deeper she felt trained and qualified to do the job. She had good appraisals and knew that she was doing her job well. She had all the skills, with good feedback. She confessed that at home she felt like an amateur, as if she didn't know what she was doing. She felt like a fish out of water.

Remember, your relationship with your child is like any other relationship. You are just slightly more attached to what they do and do not do. You may think you are failing because it's a struggle, but struggling is not failing.

So I asked Lyn, 'If there was an end result for parenting, what would it be?' 'That's easy,' she said. 'That I have raised a responsible, understand-ing and independent young man.' 'Are you responsible, understanding and independent?' I asked. 'Sure,' she replied. Having established that she was indeed qualified to do the job, I left Lyn with the homework of writing a job description for herself as a parent.

Lyn, like many parents, was parenting blindly. It is, after all, a job for which we get no instruction book or operations manual. Without any route or end destination it's not surprising that we get lost. **As a parent we must be clear about what we want and where we are going before we can even attempt to have conversations with our children.** Notice how Lyn didn't even mention the word 'respect' when I asked her about an end result of parenting.

Lyn came back with her job description written, and we compared it with what I call 'parenting patterns' – patterns of parenting that we use, whether or not they lead us where we want to go. Lyn realized that her pattern made her the victim – every time Alan did not listen or did not do as she asked, she became the victim and the 'you do not respect me' line came out. This was a pattern she noticed in her mother and she could clearly see that by assuming the victim role she was not presenting responsibility to Alan and hence was not adhering to her job description. We worked initially with three dominant patterns that Lyn felt were not serving her ultimate aim and replaced them with new patterns that she had written on her job description.

So 'victim' was changed to 'How can I make this challenge a responsibility lesson for Alan?' Every time Lyn recognized she was a victim she was to take herself away and ask herself that question.

We all have parenting patterns that we have inherited, from how we were brought up, as well as from books, the media and a multitude of other sources. We believe that something works so we try it with little thought as to whether we agree with it or if it's in line with what we think parenting is about. We each have dominant patterns and they are recognizable to us all in different ways. For me, when I am going into a victim pattern, my whole face clenches, I tighten my jaw and I begin to get a headache; that is how I know. My body tells me before my mind does and at that point I know I can choose to continue with this or I can choose a different response.

Lyn came back to the next session with what, for her, was a great win. It was Sunday and she had cooked the biggest Sunday lunch which had taken her hours. Just as it was ready Alan came down and told her he was going out. Usually Lyn would start doing her whole 'no one appreciates me, how can you do this to me?' routine. However, she stopped and asked herself, 'How can I make this challenge a respon-sibility lesson for Alan?' Instead of shouting and screaming she said, 'It's your choice, however, just so you know, I will not be cooking another meal today.' She surprised herself and Alan too, because he sat down and ate the meal.

Over the next few weeks Lyn had many tiny victories like this and gradually began to feel that she was more in control of herself and that she really was fulfilling her job description. We even gave the system she was using a name – 'Choice and State'. It was simple – whenever she felt like a victim she would always let Alan know he had a choice and state the facts.

The laundry was another good example. She would say, 'Alan, I am about to do the laundry. Can you bring your dirty clothes down?' He would say something like, 'I can't be bothered,' or 'I'm sleeping,' and she would simply say, 'You have a choice, Alan. I will not be coming up to get it and I will not be doing any more washing until Thursday.'

Not everything went swimmingly. In fact, after a few weeks of 'Choice and State' all hell broke loose. It was a laundry hell . . .

Lyn had stuck to her word and had not gone up to get the laundry and needless to say, Alan did not want to wear something that was dirty. He came down all ablaze asking her why she had not washed his favourite shirt. She explained that she had told him to bring his dirty clothes down and, as he had chosen not to, his washing had not been done. Alan was less than happy and blew up, swearing and shouting and ranting and raving, telling her to wash the shirt now. She refused, so he pushed her and ran out of the house to his friends. Lyn rang me in tears, needing some support.

The first thing I asked her was, 'What do you want to do?' Here was her first dilemma. She wanted to wash the shirt to make everything better but she knew that if she did, she was giving in and throwing away the good work she had done. She was here, after all, to teach Alan responsibility, understanding and independence and if she gave in, how would she be true to herself?

 FREEZE: WHAT WOULD YOU HAVE DONE? ....
Would you have washed the shirt?

Here was an important choice for Lyn, between help and rescue. She could take the easy and soft option by washing the shirt and rescuing him, or she could help him, which may take a little longer but would teach him more in the long run. It's so easy when we are busy, tired and drained to just rescue our children and give in. But what are they learning if we do that? When we choose rescue, we are denying our teenagers a valuable learning process. **As parents we are leaders (of our children) and as leaders we must stop doing what is easy in our lives and start doing what is right.**

Lyn decided that she would not rescue Alan and that she would help him instead. So together we worked out a system that she could apply to this and other similar situations, to enable her to help rather than rescue.

Four-Step Responsibility System

Step One – State the behaviour and tell them what they are doing.

'Alan, do you realize you are shouting at me about something that is not my fault? I want to help you but I cannot talk to you while you are shouting at me. If you stop then we can discuss it, but if you continue then I will walk away.'

Step Two – Show understanding.

'I appreciate how important this is to you and that you want the shirt now.'

Step Three – Explain the situation.

'The reason the shirt is not washed is because you did not bring it to me when I asked, and this is the result of your choice.'

Step Four – State what you will and will not do.

'I can see how important this is to you but I am not prepared to wash it for you. However, I will show you how to use the washing machine.'

Laundry hell ended with Lyn showing Alan how to use the machine and he was never late again when he was asked to bring his washing.

Lyn continued in her quest. The swearing and shouting became a weekly occurrence rather than daily and he began to do certain things without being asked (like bringing his washing to her on a Monday). Alan even began to speak in paragraphs to her and they did occasionally catch themselves giggling together. However, Lyn still felt that Alan did not show respect for her in the house and it was time for us to look at this issue. I asked Lyn one simple question: 'What do you respect about Alan?' 'Nothing,' she said. 'He is lazy and ignorant.' 'If you don't respect your own son, Lyn, how can you expect him to respect you?'

We often expect our children to be able to give us what we want (like respect) and sometimes they just don't know how, as they have never been shown. Young people these days are shown little respect from school, from the media and from society as a whole. If we cannot show them how it feels to be respected, then how on earth can we expect them to show it to us in return? We are, I think, so hung up on this word 'respect', thinking that it is something that must be earned or deserved rather than something we just get for being a human being. The definition in the dictionary quite simply relates to admiration or esteem. If we cannot hold our children in admiration, then who can?

I asked Lyn to go home and make a list of all the things that she could respect or admire in Alan, even if she did not agree with them. It was a challenging task for her. She came back saying through gritted teeth that she could admire the fact that he put himself first and that he met his own needs (a quality that she agreed she could do with more of). I challenged Lyn to tell him this, and she bravely took the challenge on.

One afternoon, when Alan eventually dragged himself out of bed, she said, 'You know Alan, I really respect the way you are so relaxed and how you are always able to put yourself first. I would love to be more like that.' After first telling her not to 'take the mickey', Alan then asked her if she had been smoking something that she shouldn't have! After she convinced him that she really meant it, he actually smiled and said, 'Thank you.' Lyn called me that day – this was the best connection she had had with Alan for years. His reaction had amazed her. Lyn continued to tell Alan what she respected about him and he began to help more around the house, get up earlier and even look at college brochures. Lyn had all the techniques she needed to continue without me. Nearly a year after I first met Lyn my work was done and she was ready to do it alone. Her biggest achievement had been in managing herself and her own emotions first so that she could then be a parent in the way she wanted. She had, first and foremost, learnt to respect herself and Alan. She was now receiving respect in return. Lyn had shown that with determination and conviction you can turn any situation round.

Recently I had this e-mail from her:

Sarah, I just want to tell you how thankful we are for all you have done for us. The other day Alan brought his girlfriend (the first one we have ever met) round for dinner. She is lovely and I am reminded that you can judge the person by the company they keep. The funny thing was that she was telling us about her dreams and plans for the future (a very dedicated young woman) and Alan looked at us and said, 'You have to respect her passion, don't you?' My husband and I just looked at each other with a secret smile. We knew we had done our job, the rest is up to him now . . . we just wanted you to know.

Action Points

....

1. Claim back the power.

Just as Lyn did, look at where you are giving your power away in waiting for someone else to change your life. It really is like waiting on the wrong side of the road and wondering why the bus is not turning up. Get your power back – don't complain and give all the responsibility to your teenager because it gives him power. Take back responsibility for yourself. You are in charge of your own actions and choices and you can take on this challenge. You can change your situation by taking action.

2. Reach into your life.

Look at your life and find the areas where you feel most powerful, and where you do not give away your power. Look at what is different for you in these situations. What makes you powerful and responsible in these situations, yet not at home? What makes you feel less powerful with your teenager? How does your teenager make you react so that you give away your power? What can you learn from these situations and carry forth into your parenting?

3. Start with the end in mind.

What do you think your job is as a parent? What are you here to do? Start by writing a job description for yourself as a parent. Lyn was clear that her job was to raise a responsible, understanding and independent young man. What do you want to do? Take a look at your answer and then ask, 'If this is the job, what is the job description and what should I be doing every day?'

4. Face the demons.

Look at the ways in which you act as a parent and see if they fit with your new job description. You may need to examine yourself for several weeks as you may not be aware of what the habits are. Notice what happens that makes you angry or sad as a parent. What happens in your body before you shout, scream or cry?

Extract the top three parenting patterns that you don't like and look at the reasons why you use them and where they come from. When I use my 'victim pattern' it enables me to blame and not be responsible and I therefore do not have to take action.

Which parenting patterns are you going to ditch? Which are going to stay? How do you know you are going into an unsuitable parenting pattern and what can you do to get yourself out of it?

5. Start taming your teenager.

Use the 'Choice and State' technique with your teenager. Make a list of all the things that you want to be different in the house and start with something small. So if your teenager decides not to tidy his room, tell him it is his choice and then state the consequence of that choice. For example, 'If you choose not to tidy your room I will be unable to get the washing and therefore you will have no clean clothes.' Harsh as it may seem, you are simply teaching them how the world works.

6. Choose help over rescue.

Decide you will not choose the easy option, you will choose what is right for you, your family and your teenager. To rescue is to bring out of danger, to help is to give aid and to encourage. There may be a time when you need to 'rescue' your teenager, there may be a time when he is in real danger, but this will be rare. Think about what help means. Make time to teach your child what it is and what it feels like to be helped. If you continue to rescue him, you are allowing him to miss out on learning opportunities. So next time he asks you for a fiver, before you reach into your pocket, ask yourself, 'Am I helping him or rescuing him?' It is all right to say, 'I am not prepared to give you that money but what I can do is help you to get it another way.' Make it a priority to give your teenager the time and don't settle for the fast and easy option. Think three-course meal, not fast food – which is more nourishing and sustaining?

7. Four-Step Responsibility System

When things get a little heated, stay calm, remember what your job is as a parent and follow Lyn's four-step approach. Don't forget to encourage natural consequences.

8. Don't diss me.

Be brave, start showing your teenager that you respect him. Behave towards him in the way you want him to behave towards you. Remember that respect is something that must be learnt, and to teach it to our children we must show it ourselves. Respect is defined as holding someone in high esteem – don't you, as the parent, want to do this? Make a list of all the things you can respect about your teenager. Make a commitment to tell him daily one thing you respect about him.

2

My teenager is not taking on any responsibility

She has to be reminded of things over and over, day after day – clean your teeth, tidy your room, do your chores, take your books to school, the list is endless and repetitive. Help!

In this chapter I will show you how to help your child to take responsibility for the everyday things in life which need to be done, so that you can ease the stress and stop the arguments. It can be the most annoying and frustrating part of bringing up teenagers. I don't think I have ever met a parent who told me that her teenager (or even child for that matter) took responsibility without a struggle.

I think we have to accept that no one likes doing chores. To expect a child to happily skip and do them would be unreasonable and downright impossible. So when you read this chapter, instead of thinking, 'How can I make my child want to do her chores?' try thinking, 'How can I teach my child about responsibility?'

We will follow Jo's journey as she helps her daughter Susie to take responsibility.

Case Study: Jo and Susie

....

Jo and her fifteen-year-old daughter Susie had a good relationship and most of the time all was well. However, there was one hurdle in the house, one bone of contention, one thing that they constantly argued about and yes, you've guessed it – it was chores! Every morning Jo was nagging at Susie, 'Have you done this, have you done that, have you packed this, have you packed that, have you fed the cats, have you brushed your teeth?' Jo was exhausted. She had tried everything – leaving her notes, doing a conventional chore board, punishing, rewarding – and nothing had worked. It did not matter what she did, the situation appeared to go from bad to worse.

The battle in this household is quite typical. Susie has moved into the teenage years and Jo is still treating her as a child. Susie is growing up and changing, her brain is now able to deal with much more complex thoughts and ideas and she needs to be managed less. Jo is still in her managing role and is still reminding Susie of everything. Susie wants more independence as she grows up to be an adult and does not want to be reminded every five minutes to clean her teeth, put her books in her school bags, etc. The more Susie is reminded, the more irritated and annoyed she becomes. The more Susie knows Jo will remind her, the more she will refuse to take responsibility. This is a real 'Catch 22' situation.

Jo needs to understand that her constant reminding is part of the problem. Another part of the problem is that Jo is not clear in her own mind why she is doing what she does. Is it for Susie's benefit or is it partly for Jo's benefit as well? Perhaps she does it so that people won't think she is a bad parent.

Youngsters need to learn about taking responsibility for their own actions. They have to find out the hard way that their actions will sometimes result in there being 'a price to pay'.

I asked Jo, 'Who does it affect if Susie does not clean her teeth and put the correct book in her bag?' She quickly said, 'Well, her of course. She is the one that smells, she is the one that will get into trouble at school,' she paused, 'but I don't want people thinking that I have a smelly daughter who cannot organize herself.' 'So who are you reminding her for?' I asked. 'I guess I am reminding her for me, I am worried how it reflects on me.' . . . BINGO!

Jo needed to hand some responsibilities over to Susie and let her be responsible for her own actions. Susie needed to learn for herself what the consequences might be whenever she got things wrong. I asked Jo to make a list of all the things that Susie could take responsibility for herself. Things like cleaning herself, packing her school bag. I then told her to say to Susie, 'I think it is about time that you took responsibility for these things yourself and then I will not be "nagging" you about them anymore.' It was also important for Jo to say one final thing – 'If you need any help, come and ask me.'

When we hand responsibility over to our children for things we have been nagging them about it is important that we find out what help they need. This is why I suggested to Jo that she should reassure Susie that if she wanted help she only had to ask.

When they mess up, don't chastise them. Ask what they think

they need to do next time so that it does not happen again. Remember that up until now no one has taught them how to organize and take care of their responsibilities. If they mess up it does not mean they are lazy. It is just that they have not yet found a system that works for them. Help them to find a better way of doing it.

Jo told Susie that she was going to stop nagging her and trust her to do certain things herself. Susie (as I anticipated) did little to respond. She just acknowledged her and said, 'All right then.' Jo found it hard but she did her best in the morning not to stand behind Susie and nag her about everything while she was getting ready; she left her to it, however hard it was. In fact she found that by leaving her alone she got an extra thirty minutes in bed so she took that time to relax more in the mornings and do some reading! Mornings had become less of a battle and as the days went on Jo felt less anxious and stayed out of Susie's way more.

After a few weeks things took a turn for the worse. One day Susie came home with a letter stating that she had a detention for not bringing the correct text books into school on the correct day. Jo rang me in a panic about what she should do.

 FREEZE: WHAT WOULD YOU HAVE DONE? ·········
Would you have grounded Susie? Shouted at her? Called the school to find out more about the situation?

Following Jo's panic call, I said to her, 'How about if instead of seeing this as a problem we see it as a learning opportunity?' – stunned silence. 'What is the opportunity here?' I asked. Again a few moments of silence, and then a reply, 'I guess there is an opportunity for me to teach her how to organize herself.' 'Well done,' I said. 'So here is what I want you to do. I want you to go to Susie and implement a four-step "learn and consequence" system. Here is how it will work.' I outlined the following list:

1. Tell her that this detention is a consequence of her own actions, of not organizing herself.
2. Ask her what she can do to ensure it does not happen again.
3. Help her to put a system in place.
4. Ask her what she has learnt.

Jo did exactly that and after an hour she and Susie together came up with a colour-coded system that allowed Susie to remember each day what books she had to take. Susie even appeared to enjoy making up the system and said she had learnt that there were consequences to her actions and that what she needed for support were systems.

The only real and tangible way to manage responsibility in a home is with effective systems. Most parents, when they are thinking of giving their children jobs or chores, dictate to them what they will and will not do; they make up the system and give it to them. **If you want your child to take ownership of the system and 'buy' into it then you need to involve her in the creation of it.**

Jo began to feel a sense of relief, they argued less about the little things and Susie began to take more responsibility. It felt as if it was now time to move on, give Susie more responsibility and tackle the bigger problem of household chores.

When it comes to your child taking responsibility it really is an opportunity to teach them how things are in the real world. In the real world we make agreements with people every day, agreements about when we will pay our mortgage, when we will start work, where we will meet our friends for lunch. Some of these agreements can be negotiated; for example, what time we meet a friend, but some are non-negotiable like paying our mortgage. We take responsibility for our part in the agreement. Deciding which chores your child will be responsible for is just like making agreements in real life. It is giving them a valuable lesson in life too.

 TIME OUT ··
After helping parents and teenagers with countless systems about responsibility in the home, I have found the most effective ones with teenagers involve money. There are two advantages. First, you have them interested since you are talking about money. Secondly, you are killing two birds with one stone by teaching them also about the importance of managing and earning money. I call this the 'Money for Chores' system and it is very easy to manage. Take the amount that you normally give your teenager for pocket money and divide it by four. Give her one quarter of the amount to start with. She can do what she wishes with it, it

cannot be taken away for failure to do jobs or for bad behaviour. It is hers to keep. The other three quarters she has to earn by doing a number of jobs which are worth a certain amount of money each.

....

We decided to introduce the 'Money for Chores' system but we needed to make sure that Susie could buy into it and feel she was involved in the creation of it. If Jo was to just approach Susie and tell her that this was the new system and that she had to stick to it, the reaction would be pretty obvious. Instead, Jo needed to approach Susie with a request and make it very clear that they would come to an agreement together. So here is what I left Jo doing. She had to say to Susie, 'Susie, I want to set up a different system for your pocket money. You will get £5 which will be yours for keeps, to use as you wish. The rest of the money you will earn by doing a series of jobs. Each job will be worth £3 if done consistently every week for a month. I want you to think about what jobs you would like to be responsible for and then we will speak about it tomorrow night.' Note here how Jo gave Susie a time to discuss this. She didn't want her to have any 'wriggle' room, as she knew that the next night they would be discussing this, whether Susie liked it or not. . . . As you can imagine, Susie was less than happy and refused to discuss the matter at all with her mum. Jo just said, 'Susie, you have a choice. You can agree with me about the jobs you want to be responsible for or I can pick the jobs for you. I will be putting this system into operation and you will not receive more than £5 a month unless you do jobs to earn it.' It was very hard for Jo to be so direct and straight with her daughter; however, she knew that it was necessary. Eventually, Susie said she would sit down and discuss the matter. Jo now needed to go through the 'agreement system' with Susie to ensure they came to a clear and concise result.

The agreement system is a simple three-step approach.

Step One – Be clear.

Be clear about the result you want.

Jo wanted Susie to take some responsibility for chores in the house in return for money. Ideally there would be five chores at £3 each, done weekly and consistently, that would add up to £15. She wanted these chores to be something that she would normally do herself and not something that did not need to be done.

Step Two – Make the request and negotiate.

Make the request by outlining what you want to do and *ask* for an agreement to be discussed and reached.

When Jo asked Susie what she wanted to take responsibility for the answer was 'nothing'. Jo then asked what she was willing to do in exchange for money. Again, Susie said 'nothing'.

FREEZE: WHAT WOULD YOU HAVE DONE? ·········

Would you have shouted? Would you have said, 'Right, fine, then you get no money ever'? Or would you have panicked, just like Jo did?

Jo called me in a panic and I had to point out that since she had asked, she had to be ready for the 'no'. As with any request, you are giving your child the chance to say 'no', so be prepared for it.

They went through a very tense few months with Susie not doing anything and constantly nagging Jo for money. Jo remained strong and stuck to her word, and did not give Susie a penny more. If she had, then Susie would have won and Jo would have no sense of power or authority within the house. Halfway through month three Susie came to Jo and said, 'Okay, I am now willing to earn money for jobs, can we go back to that thing you were talking about?'

Sticking to what you say and being consistent is so important here; otherwise everything becomes ineffective. The minute you give in is the minute you have undone all the hard work.

Step Three – Seal the deal.

You and your teenager must both be clear about *what* is to be done, and *when* it is to be done. A useful ploy is to write it down, make lists.

39

Susie decided on five jobs: cleaning her bedroom, vacuuming the house, taking out the rubbish, cooking a meal one night a week and cleaning the bathroom. Jo was happy with what Susie had chosen. Before they could cement their agreements they had to make sure that they both clearly understood their decisions and the time involved.

For each job they wrote out a little card, stating exactly what was required. Only when they had done that did Jo say the all-important words that would seal the deal. She needed to be very clear so that there was no 'wriggle' room. If we take the rubbish, for example, Jo said, 'So we have an agreement that every Thursday morning you will have the rubbish outside the front door by 8am. This needs to be done every week and a failure to do it will mean that you don't earn the money for it.' She was clear that Susie had agreed with them all and any final negotiations were completed. When they were both happy Jo asked one final thing, 'What help do you need?' 'Well, I might need reminding,' Susie said. Jo was quick to hand back responsibility to Susie. She asked her what she could do to remind herself to do the chores. Susie chose a system that was similar to the one they had put in place with the books. It was a colour-coded chart that showed which jobs had to be done on each day of the week and it had a place for her mum to tick when each job had been completed. Susie also asked her mum to remind her whenever a job had not been done.

Here is the chart Susie produced.

Susie's Chore Board

Day	Job	Complete
Monday	Bedroom	
Tuesday	Meal	
Wednesday	Bathroom	
Thursday	Rubbish	
Friday	Vacuum	

Every evening Jo checked the chart and if the job was done she ticked the box. If it was not, she reminded Susie. When Susie did not do her job one week she did not get the money. It did not mean that Susie did not sometimes ask her mum for more money and when she did, it was for Jo to decide. Sometimes she would give it and sometimes she would suggest another job in return for the £3. Jo found that as the system was used more she found herself reminding Susie less and eventually, if Susie wanted some more money she would offer a job that she could do for it. They still had some arguments and Susie did not always do everything. But Jo felt 100 per cent better and it was time for me to back off. Jo had stopped nagging and was allowing Susie to take responsibility for herself.

This whole process took about six months to complete and I can report that Jo and Susie are still doing well. Susie has really taken to the colour-coded system she created and even has one for her homework now. Jo has found that by putting these systems in place and 'backing off' Susie, she has so much extra time to herself that she is now doing some of the things that she did not have time for before.

Action Points

1. Hand it over.

Go through your day and make a note of all the things you are doing for your teenager. Which of these could you hand over so that you could teach her more about responsibility? Also, look at the financial support you are giving. Could that change in the light of what you have read in this chapter? Could you implement the 'Money for Chores' system? If you are finding this difficult, make a list of all the things that you are nagging your teenager about – the things that seem like a constant struggle – and start there.

2. Stop managing and start handing over responsibility.

Decide that from this day forth you will no longer manage your teenager; you will no longer check her every five minutes to make sure that she has brushed her teeth. The manager is fired! Let her make her own mistakes, let her learn and be herself. Hand one thing over to her today, sit down and tell her what you are doing, and ask her what she wants to be responsible for.

3. When she makes a mess of things (which she will) use the 'learn and consequence' system.

Point out the consequence: calmly let your teenager know the consequence of her action or inaction. For example, 'You were late for school today, so for the rest of this week I will decide what time you go to bed.'

Ask what she can do to make sure it will not happen again.

Help her to find a solution: don't take over, but offer ideas and suggestions.

Ask her what she has learnt: this one is really important if you want to make sure that the same mistakes are not made again.

4. Decide not to see mistakes as failure but as learning opportunities.

When your child makes a mistake ask her what she has learnt and move on.

5. Start a new system that takes into account jobs for money.

Change your attitude towards how pocket money is given in the house. You have to work for your money, so should your teenager. Speak with your teenager about what you can put in place. Will it be jobs for money or will it be something else?

6. Know the results you want to achieve.

Be clear about what results you want as a parent before you go into any negotiations with your teenager. It is important that you know the limit of your negotiation. Your teenager will pick up on any inconsistencies and you will feel that she has got one over on you.

7. Make agreements.

Make agreements with your teenager about her responsibilities using these three steps:

- Know the result you want.
- Make a request and enter into negotiations.
- Come to an agreement and seal the deal.

8. Systems, systems, systems.

Help your teenager to come up with a system that works for her. Without a system you and she may fail. Don't take over, just help and offer suggestions. Remember that teenagers do not know how to organize themselves and you will be teaching them.

9. Sit back and enjoy yourself.

Make all this worth your while too. Think of what you are going to do with the extra time you now have. What is the one thing you have been putting off that you now have the time to do? Go and do it!

3

My teenager has no enthusiasm for school and never does his homework

He fails tests and is extremely disorganized. He offers excuse after excuse, along with an unhelpful attitude.

The purpose of this chapter is to show you how to motivate your teenager at school, get more involved in his schoolwork and put systems in place that help you both. There are so many reasons why children fail at school: their creativity; their talkative nature; the fact that they cannot see the link between the school and their future, or that their talents are not easily recognized by a system that seems to be only about grades and achievement.

School can be a very stressful time for some teenagers, with some finding it a real struggle. How many of us want to come home from an eight-hour shift and then do another four hours of work? With a little planning and some creativity you can, as a parent, motivate even the most apathetic teenager. It is your job, after all, to ensure that they do as well as they can while also recognizing that ultimately it is up to them. No amount of cajoling by you will make them work harder. It has to come from within.

While school is important we should also remember that grades are only one part of the equation and that many people do extremely well without high marks. Qualities such as persistence and commitment are just as important.

During this chapter we will follow Chrissie as she tries to curb her son Louis and his wayward tendencies.

Case Study: Chrissie and Louis

Louis (thirteen) was a true joker, he made everyone laugh and could get along with almost anyone. All the teachers liked him but comments like 'lazy' and 'needs to try harder' would always appear on his report card. Chrissie, a single mum, was at her wits end. It didn't seem to matter what she did, Louis had no regard for school or his work and as far as he was concerned school was a place to socialize. He was diagnosed as dyslexic and was in classes at school far below his intelligence. He challenged the teachers and was regularly in trouble. At home he had a large number of friends and he was always coming up with hair-brained schemes like leasing his books to his friends for money, typing people's work on the computer for money, buying and selling things on eBay. He was always after making a quick buck and was fearless in his nature. He never did his homework and never studied.

It was obvious to me that Louis was highly gifted, a real opportunistic individual. I saw it so often when I was in the police. Gifted, sociable teenagers who could sell snow to an Eskimo yet could not spell, did not like school and had incredibly quick minds when it came to ideas and problem solving. What we needed to do in order to motivate Louis was to find out what drives him and where his true passion lies.

When Chrissie first came to me she could see nothing good about Louis and his behaviour. It did not matter how much she told Louis that school was important, nothing seemed to change. The first thing I had Chrissie do was make a list of all the things that she thought were bad about Louis. It was a long list and included things like lazy, deceitful and arrogant. I then asked her to take the list away and turn each negative thing she had written into a positive one. For example, what was good about him being lazy, what was good about him being deceitful and so on. She went away apprehensive to say the least.

A week later she came back with her list and she had done a good job. Lazy had become laid back, deceitful had become intelligent and arrogant had become confident. She even said to me, 'Sarah, I have a talented son, thank you for helping me to see that. Now what do I do with him?' Good question, I thought. The next thing we needed to do was help Louis to see that he was clever and talented. We had to boost his self-esteem so we could start to help him in a different way. I gave Chrissie some simple homework. Every time that Louis did something she would have disapproved of previously she was now to praise what was good about it.

When Chrissie came back she was smiling. 'You will never guess what,' she said. 'Last week they put Louis in charge of the tuck shop and he has already found a cheaper supplier and increased profits by twenty per cent. He is now talking about how the school can use the money to buy scoobies to sell on for a profit in the dining hall.' There was no denying it now, Louis was a talented lad. Chrissie was certainly seeing Louis in a different light. Previously, she would have criticized him for making such a fuss, now she was enjoying the ride with him. The only thing left for us now was to get Louis to see it and to apply this creativity to his school work. Every time Louis did something similar, Chrissie was saying things like, 'How creative,' or 'What good problem solving skills you have.' She was beginning to put a name to his previously unnamed characteristics. Chrissie and Louis had more conversations about his schemes and plans and how he could recognize opportunities that others could not see, and about the amount of persistence and tenacity it took to carry them out. Chrissie even caught Louis watching an episode of *The Apprentice* on TV, telling the candidates what they were doing wrong. He proudly declared to Chrissie, 'I want to be like that, I want to be as successful as Alan Sugar.' Bingo, we had a way in! We had found the motivation required to help Louis to succeed. By observing Louis and engaging with him, Chrissie had found her way in. Now all we had to do was link this to his school work.

What we must remember is that each child is different and each child needs motivating in a different way. Louis was not motivated by the promise of good grades or the threat of bad ones, but by opportunities and risk. So when motivating him we needed to look at how these two factors could be brought into the equation.

In our next session Chrissie and I talked about each school subject that Louis took and how we could put the element of risk and opportunity into it. Maths was easy as we could relate it to running a business, History had us putting Louis in parliamentary power, science had us talking about how the scientific breakthrough he was about to make was life or death, and so on. We carried on through each subject using our own thoughts, although we knew the real test was to give the power to Louis. We decided to start with his worst subject, History. As it happened, they were studying the Second World War and we thought that was an excellent place to start. First, Chrissie called the school to see when the next history homework was due, which was Tuesday, so that night, when Louis came in from school, she asked if she could look at his history homework. Louis got it out with a succession of moans and groans – it was something about Churchill. Chrissie read the piece of homework and simply said, 'You know that Churchill was a great man, he could see an opportunity and he was a real risk-taker – what opportunities do you think he did not take?' That was it, she had him, he was all over his History homework. She had inspired him in the way he needed to be inspired. He did his homework in record time and got a 'C' for it, which after all the 'Es' and 'Fs' was a good result. We had made a start, found a way to motivate Louis, but we still had a long way to go.

It was time that we devised a simple system to help Chrissie to keep track of his schoolwork and homework. For this I enlisted the help of a great friend of mine, Chris Sfassie, the creator of an organization tool for teenagers called the Grade Maker (www.grade-maker.com). The Grade Maker is a simple file system that has daily, weekly and monthly repeat task sheets in it. The parent or the teenager writes on these sheets the things that need to be done daily, weekly and monthly and at the end of the day the child ticks them off and brings the file to the parent to check.

Chrissie first of all asked the school for a breakdown of the subjects, to find out what was due and when. For example, she knew that on Monday he had Humanities homework and it was due in on Wednesday. She wrote on the weekly task sheets what was due weekly. She presented the Grade Maker file to Louis and said, 'Louis, I really want you to succeed at school and in life so you can take over Alan Sugar's empire. What I know is that to run a successful business you must be organized and deliver things when you have said you would. I want to introduce this system into the house.' She explained the system to him and, as you can guess, he was less than happy and moaned, grunted and slammed a few doors. All of this was okay, I just told Chrissie to ignore how he behaved towards it and just check it every night to see if he had done what he was supposed to do. She did this every night for two weeks and Louis simply would not have anything to do with it. If anything he was worse. It was time for some tough action.

We needed to give Louis a reason to become interested and a reason to actually pick up the book and start to do his homework. Taking responsibility was the route that we followed and we decided to link the homework issue with the fact that he was not taking responsibility. So every time he asked to do something that required an element of responsibility, like going to a party, staying out late, asking for more money to start another one of his schemes, Chrissie was simply to say, 'Louis, until you can show me that you can take responsibility for your school work I cannot give you responsibility in other areas.' After about ten times of repeating this he finally got the message. He came home from school one night, stomped into his bedroom, stayed there for about an hour and then came down with his Grade Maker file to show his mum he had done what he was supposed to. He continued to do this reluctantly for about two weeks, moaning and groaning, but Chrissie just ignored it. He then stopped moaning and his school grades gradually began to rise and the reports from his teachers improved. As he took more responsibility with his school work Chrissie gave him more responsibility in other areas. She occasionally asked him if he needed any help and most of the time he said, 'No.' When he did she simply went back to the earlier system they had created and appealed to his opportunistic and risk-taking nature. All was going well until one day . . .

Louis came home shouting and swearing and banging around . . . he was angry. Chrissie asked him what was wrong and he just declared that he was not going to school any more, it was stupid and he couldn't see the point. 'I am not going,' he screamed, 'and there is nothing you can do about it.'

 FREEZE: WHAT WOULD YOU HAVE DONE? ·········
Would you have screamed at him? Told him he was going whether he liked it or not? Panicked as Chrissie did and called me?

Chrissie called me and I went round. It transpired that one of his teachers had called him stupid and told him that he would never succeed in life. Louis thought he was no good at anything and said he might as well give in. Chrissie was distraught. After all the hard work we had done Louis was back at square one. It was time to rethink. I advised her to contact the school immediately and speak with them about the situation as it was totally inappropriate for a teacher to do this.

One comment can have such a profound effect on young people, especially if it comes from a teacher. Often, what can happen at school is that we are judged on our ability to perform to a set of pre-defined standards and it is through these standards that it is decided whether we are bright or not, whether we are intelligent or not. However, the work by Howard Garner in *Frames of Mind* shows us that there are several intelligences and his work on multiple intelligences has opened up a whole new field of thinking about intelligence and smartness. I prefer to call these intelligences 'senses' and they are described below:

Word sense

This is the ability to read and write words well, possessed by someone who would do well at school. It is one of the means by which we currently measure IQ. It is also the sense we are all aware of and which may cause us to panic or to try to remedy if our child appears not to show it.

Number sense

This is being good or clever with numbers. People with this sense are likely to be very good at Maths and to have an interest in money and the way finances work.

Picture Sense

This is creative and is seen in the child who makes and designs things, always creating and drawing. People possessing this sense see the world in pictures.

Body Sense

Athletes and dancers display this sense; they use their bodies to get ahead, they learn by hands-on methods. Youngsters who are good at visual and practical things and who gravitate towards cookery and woodwork classes also show it.

Self Sense

This enables people to manage their emotions and motivate themselves. They are good at achieving goals they set for themselves.

People Sense

This gives people the ability to talk, communicate and 'schmooze' with great ease, often being charismatic and good at speaking. This sense enables people to be very sociable and usually to be liked by everyone.

Nature Sense

This is displayed in those with a natural gift for dealing with plants and animals.

When we realize that there is more than one way to be clever, it opens up new possibilities and allows us to see options that were not apparent before.

When we teach teenagers about this we help them to make sense of themselves and the world around them and, when someone calls them stupid again, they know it is not true.

I went through this concept with both Chrissie and Louis and I could see his eyes lighting up. Something in him was awakening and it was encouraging to see. He looked at the list for a long time and decided that indeed he was intelligent and he had people sense and body sense. Louis could suddenly see that there was hope and the temporary 'glitch' was overcome as he went to school with the knowledge that he was indeed smart. He continued to work well, he was still Louis with strange ideas, but he concentrated more on what was important to him – becoming like Alan Sugar! All was well until exam time came around. Louis called me in a panic: he wanted to do well but he really had no idea how best to study, so I spent a day with him.

When studying, you are fighting a losing battle if you cannot understand the best way in which you take in information and remember it. I frequently use the teaching of the Highland Ability Battery, which helps us to identify our main learning styles. They are:

Reading and Writing

From your early days at school and right through life you learn by reading and writing. This is why it is the style or method mostly taught and used in school. The experts give this style the name 'Verbal Memory' because it is all to do with words.

Listening

This style is known as 'Tonal Memory' and is the one preferred by people who learn most easily by hearing. When in class they are likely to enjoy discussions, where there are people talking. They are not so attentive when there is writing to be done. When studying they may read and talk out loud or record themselves and listen at a later date, or they may want a background of music. They will also ask others to question them so they can speak their answers.

Doing

This style is known as 'Rhythm Memory' and is a great help to people who learn best when they are involved in some kind of movement at the same time. These will be the students constantly fidgeting at school, who cannot sit still. When studying they are likely to walk around and make up rhythmic songs and poems. These students may benefit from studying with either the TV or radio on, and also may hum or sing while they are studying.

Graphics

This style is known as 'Design Memory' – preferred by people who learn most easily when they can see or draw pictures, tables or graphs. When studying, they are likely to draw pictures and put information into tables and boxes.

We decided that Louis was high in rhythm and tonal memory and therefore his previous attempts to study, which had involved sitting alone in a room, had been unsuccessful. He needed to move around and speak. Together, Louis and I worked out three ways that would help him. One, he would speak the work into a dictaphone and listen to it on his way to and from school. Two, he would make up songs while playing his guitar, to help him learn, and then his mum would test him. Three, we worked out a system that would help him get organized with his study. It was a simple colour-coded system that required a file, some books and index cards in corresponding colours. Each subject was given a colour. For example, geography was blue. He would write geography notes in his blue book and then transfer the things he needed to remember onto the blue cards. These are what he would study from and be tested on. The blue file was for any other information and loose pieces of paper he needed to keep for geography. The system seemed to work well and Louis kept on top of things, steadily improving his test scores.

Louis and Chrissie's journey took eighteen months but it was in time for Louis to leave school. He left with good results. He failed in some subjects but on the whole he did what he needed to and is now studying business at college. He still has bizarre schemes and is at present designing websites for his friends in return for drinks in the bar.

Action Points

....

1. Change the way you see your teenager.

No doubt, if your teenager does have tendencies like Louis, he is driving you mad and is in trouble a lot. First, you need to change your own way of looking at situations. When you do this, you will change how you behave towards him and that in turn will make him feel better, raise his self-esteem and may even make him like school more. Write a list of all the things you think that he is bad at and turn them into positives.

2. Inspiration and beyond!

Find out what or who motivates your teenager, talk to the teachers and have discussions with them about how you can inspire him to reach his full potential. Help him to work out how his school work can link to the vision he has of himself in the future.

3. Be wise, be smart.

Work with your teenager to find out where his senses lie, which of the senses fit him best. What impact will these have on his schoolwork?

4. What is his learning style?

Help your teenager to work out how he learns best and which way he can study best. Help him to work out better ways for doing his homework and studying.

5. Grades are only one part of the equation.

Remember that grades are only one part of who your teenager is. There is so much more to him than just his report card.

6. Become organized.

Organization is the key to any improvement at school. Help your teenager by showing him ways and methods that will enable him to get the best out of himself.

4

My teenager and I are not able to communicate

It feels as if I am lecturing her every day and I am just becoming more and more annoyed. We are drifting apart.

In this chapter I will show you how to communicate with your child so that the simple everyday things become easier to negotiate. Parents can find the transition to the teenage years difficult. From being with a child who told us everything and wanted us to go everywhere with her, we are suddenly faced with a young person who is becoming more independent and is pulling away from us.

Without good communication the parent/teenager relationship can become impossible to manage. How do you keep communications open so that you can maintain the relationship with your child while still honouring her new-found independence?

We will follow Tracy's journey as she attempts to put her relationship with her daughter Emma back on course.

Case Study: Tracy and Emma

Tracy and Emma, who is fourteen, had always had a good relationship as a single mother with one daughter. Tracy felt that the bond between them was very strong. They shared everything and spent a lot of time together – just talking. It was a very happy household. Then suddenly things changed! Emma spent more and more time alone in her room, she became much more secretive and was annoyed when Tracy asked questions about her life. She refused to answer her mother. Any answers she did give were little more than a succession of grunts. This drove Tracy to despair and usually ended up with her shouting, 'You will speak to me!' Tracy felt out of touch with her daughter. She was convinced that Emma was up to something.

As their relationship gradually deteriorated, Tracy began to feel useless as a mother. She would smile when she talked about their previous bond and all the things they did together.

'We were like best friends,' Tracy said to me in one session, and this is where a big alarm bell went off for me.

When parents become friends to their children, they find it increasingly difficult to act like parents when required; for example, when they need to tell them off about something. Yes, you can have fun, yes, you can share things but no, you cannot be just friends. Your job is to be a *parent*, not just a *friend*. Our friends do not cook our meals, do our washing, give us money, tell us off and have to keep us. *Parent* as *friend* is not a healthy combination. Similarly, at the other extreme, neither is *parent* as *dictator* (a parent who treats the house like a well-oiled business machine, barking orders). It is better to be somewhere in between — something that my great friend Diana Haskins calls *parent* as *coach*.

I said to Tracy, 'Is that your job, to be your daughter's friend?' Her face went blank. 'I am not sure I understand,' she said. 'Well how, as a friend, can you also be a parent? How can you slip from being a friend one moment to having to tell Emma to do the washing up in another? It is confusing for you and for her.' She was still not convinced so I sent Tracy away to make two lists. On one she was to write all the things a friend would do for someone and on the other she was to write all the things a parent would do. She went away and came back after a week with a long face. 'I have done my lists,' she said, 'and the trouble is I want to be both, but I can see that both does not work, both is not what my daughter requires from me.'

TIME OUT

As your child progresses into the teenage years your style as a parent needs to progress too. For Tracy that was to move from friend to coach. For most it will be to move from a managing role (managing your child's day-to-day activities and checking they have done what they are supposed to do) to a coaching role (giving your child more responsibility and independence). The manager has been fired and a new job is required.

Tracy was now ready to take on a new role in her relationship with Emma – the *coach* role. Together we made a list of the top five things that this new coach/parent would do.

The list was as follows:

1. As a coach I will always respect my daughter and the decisions she makes, even if I do not agree with them.
2. As a coach I will listen to my daughter at all times.
3. As a coach I will, in all situations, attempt to understand my daughter's point of view.
4. At all times I will encourage my daughter to be responsible.
5. As a coach I will honour my daughter's need for independence.

We had defined a new role, a role that would allow her to grow with her daughter and allow her daughter to become a responsible and independent young adult. Tracy was happy with her new job description and was ready to go.

What still concerned me, though, was how negative Tracy was about her daughter. I could not help but wonder if this was having an effect on their relationship. Although she was ready to adopt this new coaching role she was still judging her daughter, calling her a good-for-nothing and lazy. This was not very coach-like!

How we see our teenagers will have an impact on how we behave towards them and ultimately how they behave towards us. There is a correlation between what we think and what appears before us. If I think you are lazy and a good-for-nothing, guess how you will show up in front of me. Yes, you will appear lazy and good-for-nothing. If I think you are helpful and kind then guess how I will see you. Yes, helpful and kind. It is a little like a self-fulfilling prophecy. If I think and tell you that you are bad all the time, then you will become bad. Similarly, if I think you are good, then guess how you will be. Think and behave differently towards your teenager and you will start to see different results. This quote from Wayne Dwyer says it all: 'Show me your circumstances and I will show you not who you are but who you think you are.'

I asked her another question. 'Tracy, when your daughter walks through the door, what do you think to yourself?' That was easy. She came out with an array of things (some of them not suitable for this book), the gist of them being, 'Oh no, here comes trouble, I wonder what mood she is in today!' So I asked Tracy, 'Do you feel that your thinking that way is having an effect on how you behave towards her?' She told me Emma made her feel she was walking on egg shells. 'It makes me snap at her, it makes me feel put upon.' 'So if you are behaving like that, what is the behaviour you are getting back?' 'Well,' she said, 'she is ignoring me, being mean, not speaking, and being rude.' Tracy had got it! She could see that what she was telling herself was having an impact on how she behaved and in return how Emma behaved towards her. 'So let's find another approach,' I said. 'Let us imagine that you are making a film and you are writing the script for when Emma comes home from school – what would you like to happen?' 'Well, I would like her to come up to me smiling, give me a hug, tell me she has had a lovely day, let me know what she would be doing that evening and then help me cook dinner.' 'Well done!' I said. 'What do you think the mother in your script is thinking just before her daughter comes home from school?' 'I am so excited to see my daughter, she is so kind, helpful and fun to be with.'

63

'That's good!' I said. 'We have found your new approach.' The homework I gave Tracy was for two weeks. Simply, she had to say this new line over and over again to herself just before Emma was about to come home, and not do anything differently. It did not matter if she believed it or not, she was just to say it.

For two weeks Tracy did exactly what she was told and reluctantly told herself that her daughter was kind and helpful. For the first three days nothing happened at all. The fourth day she shocked herself by joyfully saying, 'Hi Emma, hope you had a lovely day,' as soon as Emma walked through the door, and she continued this for the rest of the time. On day eight Emma came into her and said, 'Yes I did, thanks Mum.' On day twelve when Emma walked through the door she said, 'Hi Mum, I had a great day,' before Tracy had even had time to get her words out. When Tracy came back I said to her, 'How do you see your daughter now?' 'I see her as helpful, kind and fun,' she said. 'I am not there 100 per cent but I am getting there.' I felt it was time to move on.

Tracy's mindset towards her daughter was now much more positive so we could move on to helping her to adapt to the new coach role she had assigned to herself. We looked at Tracy's job description and moved on to her first point:

1. As a coach I will always respect my daughter and the decisions she makes, even if I do not agree with them.

Respect is an essential quality for us to cultivate in our children and one of the best ways to encourage this is to *show* respect. Only when we show respect can we expect to receive it. There are many ways that parents can show respect for their children. As parents we do not tell our children often enough what it is that we respect about them. We find it easy to tell them how proud we are of what they have done but have great difficulty in telling them how much we respect their innate qualities as humans. There is a huge difference between a parent saying, 'I am so proud you passed your exams,' and 'I really respect the commitment and dedication it took you to pass your exams.' There is a huge difference between me saying to you, 'Great job, you bought my book,' and 'I really respect the commitment you have shown to your teenager in buying this book.'

Since Tracy was such a fun-loving girl we decided that we would introduce a 'respect board' into the house.

 TIME OUT ··
The respect board is a simple device that helps everyone in the house to think and feel more positively about themselves and other family members.

It has the names of all the people in the house on it. Under the names can be written, each day, something that you respect about each person.

Over the years I have done many different types of respect board – from blackboards and white boards to ideas like the one we implemented with Tracy. Really, it does not matter how you do it, it is the thinking behind it that counts. The idea is that you start doing it and then just see if your teenager joins in. Don't push it, just see what happens.

If you are not brave enough to start a respect board, try

each day to tell your teenager one thing that you respect about her. Soon it will become second nature and you will just find yourself doing it all the time.

....

Tracy and I discussed the options and she came up with this good idea. She had a wonderful picture of her and Emma from their holiday last year that they both loved. She decided to enlarge it to poster size and use post-it notes to stick on daily when she found something she could respect about Emma. She decided to put it over the kitchen table as that was the only place that Emma was guaranteed to be at least once in the day. Emma asked her why she had done it and Tracy explained. Every day without fail Tracy would write a post-it note and stick it over Emma on the picture. At first Emma appeared not to care, but Tracy did find her peeking a few times! What Tracy did notice, which was interesting, was that Emma started eating more of her meals at the table. However, Emma had not written anything back on the board yet. I told Tracy not to panic and to just keep using it.

Tracy continued to think more positively about her daughter and made sure she found something to respect about her each day. About five weeks into our coaching, Tracy called me and was in tears: she had found a note that Emma had written on the photo which said, 'Mum, I respect the way you love me.' That night Emma came home, gave her mum a hug and sat down and had a conversation with her that lasted fifteen minutes. This was a huge breakthrough. It was time for me to teach Tracy how to listen to her daughter, so she could understand her, rather than just hear what she said, so we moved on to the second point on Tracy's job description:

2. As a coach I will listen to my daughter at all times.

Hearing and listening are two different things. We all hear what our teenagers are saying but the question is, do we really listen to them? 'Hearing' is the act of perceiving sound, for example the sound somebody makes when speaking to you. 'Listening' is paying attention to what somebody is saying – concentrating on it, understanding it and absorbing it.

A frequent complaint that we get from teenagers is that they do not feel people listen to them. You may think your teenagers don't listen to you. But to be listened to yourself, you first need to listen to others by paying attention to what they are saying – concentrating on it, understanding it and absorbing it. As Steven Covey says, 'Seek first to understand and then to be understood.'

Learning to listen from your teenager's point of view (something I call 'step into my shoes' listening) requires dedication and a lot of patience. When practising this type of listening you are trying to get inside your teenager's mind, to look at the situation through her eyes, stepping into her shoes, trying to understand her interpretation of the world, how it must feel to be a teenager in today's society with all the challenges that must bring.

'Step into my Shoes' Listening is a three-step process.

Step One – Listen with your lips closed – do not comment

Stop what you are doing, turn to face your teenager and just listen.

Step Two – Ensure you are listening from the heart, be interested and concentrate

Do not pass judgement or make comment; just close your lips and nod. If your teenager stops speaking just say, 'Tell me more,' or 'Go on.'

Step Three – Understand and listen from her point of view

Imagine you have stepped into the teenager's shoes and are looking at this situation through her eyes. Respond to her in a neutral and sincere tone. Imagine how this may look from her point of view.

Tracy needed to learn to listen to her daughter in a different way. There is a difference between hearing the words and truly wanting to understand how something looks from your teenager's viewpoint. She needed to learn to listen to Emma without judgement and without offering well-meaning advice. I taught Tracy about 'Step in my Shoes' listening.

Tracy had a very difficult time listening to her daughter in the way I suggested. It did not come easily, as you can imagine. Emma would still not have more than a fifteen-minute conversation with her and Tracy desperately wanted to get her advice and her point across, particularly when Emma told her things that were upsetting. There was one occasion when Emma returned home from school crying because one of the teachers, in assembly, had called her lazy in front of the whole school year. Tracy was furious and wanted to call the school immediately and tell them this was unacceptable.

 FREEZE: WHAT WOULD YOU HAVE DONE? ⋯⋯⋯
Would you have agreed with the teacher? Called the school? Told Emma not to be so sensitive? Or like Tracy did, just listen?

3. As a coach I will, in all situations, attempt to understand my daughter's point of view.

Tracy held her tongue and just listened, stepping into her daughter's shoes and responding from there. She found herself saying things like, 'it feels so embarrassing, I can only imagine how angry you must have felt.' Tracy did not step in and tell Emma what she would have done or what she wanted to do. She just listened from Emma's point of view and Emma spoke to her for a whole hour that day. Tracy continued for another month, implementing all the things that we had discussed, and Emma spoke with her mum more and more. Tracy was happy with the progress; she felt as if she was becoming a coach. She had stopped stepping in to save her daughter and their relationship was now based more on positives than negatives. We could now move on to Tracy's final points in her job description list – to encourage responsibility and inde-pendence. For me they go hand in hand.

4. At all times I will encourage my daughter to be responsible.

5. As a coach I will honour my daughter's need for independence.

When you think of responsibility and independence I want you to think of two more things: choice and preparation for adulthood. To me, responsibility is about giving choice and allowing your teenager to be able to show you she can be responsible. Independence is about preparing her for adulthood after she has proved she can be responsible.

Tracy had previously stated that she thought her job as a parent was to encourage responsibility and nurture independence. However, the reality in the house was very different. Tracy was for the best part Emma's slave. I sent Tracy away with one thought in her mind: to look for ways during the week in which she could make Emma take more responsibility for her own life. She was to do nothing with them, just record them so we could speak about them. She came back with a huge list, from doing her own cooking to doing her own washing. The biggest revelation she had was that she could give Emma responsibility for her schoolwork and planning her future instead of nagging her about it. This meant that Tracy would stop asking what homework she had, when it had to be in, what grade she had in her last exam and what she was going to do with her future. She would just hand the responsibility to her. So that day, after school, Emma came in and gave her mum a hug, as she now did most days. She started to tell her mum about all the homework she had to do. Rather than doing her usual interrogation, Tracy just said, 'Emma you are fourteen now and I think you are old enough to take responsibility for your school work and your future, so I am going to leave you to it now. I will still check weekly that you are doing what you are supposed to do and still expect you to tell me your results.' Emma looked at her blankly. 'If you need help,' Tracy went on, 'then ask me and we will get you what you need but from now on if you fail it will be your responsibility.' Emma was stunned and did not really know what to do.

TIME OUT

Only hand responsibility for homework and school work to your child if she is reaching her potential at school. Emma was doing so and this is why we could hand over. If Emma started to fail or slip we had to take some of that responsibility back. As a parent you need to ensure you have a check system in place so that you can see that what is being done is meant to be done. With Emma, Tracy just checked her homework diary weekly to make sure that she was still on course. I have covered homework in depth in another chapter so I will not go into it in too much detail here. Just bear in mind that there is a fine line between handing over responsibility and ensuring that you still take responsibility as a parent for the work she is supposed to be doing at school.

Over the next few months Tracy continued to hand over responsibility to Emma. She handed bedtime over to Emma, but when Emma could not get up in the morning she took responsibility back for three weeks, explaining why. Every week, Tracy would ask if Emma needed any help with her responsibilities. If she did, Tracy would do all she could to get Emma what she needed, such as extra tuition, more stationery, but she still did not interfere. Gradually, Emma began to show her mum more and more that she could be responsible, so much so that Tracy began to give her more freedom, like staying out later at the weekend and staying over with friends. Emma began to see the result of showing her mum she could be responsible and therefore did it more. When Emma 'messed up' Tracy took responsibility back. Emma was learning a huge lesson about life which was that independence comes at a price. That price is responsibility.

Tracy and Emma continued to build their relationship; the respect board had become a permanent feature and although it was not used every day, at least something was there every week. They had much more in-depth conversations and at least twice a week they would have a long meal together and a chat. Tracy continued to teach Emma about responsibility and independence, even when she did not like it. It was time for me to back off for a while and leave them to it. I left Tracy for six months to see how she got on. She had all the skills she needed now to carry on for herself.

During those six months I did not hear anything from Tracy, which told me that things were going well. When I did hear from her she had nothing but praise for her daughter. Amazing things had happened. Their communication and relationship were ten times better and Tracy was now very clear she was a Parent Coach not a Parent Friend. Emma had taken responsibility for her life and is at present on placement with a PR company to see if this is the right job for her. She had done three similar placements with the help of Tracy. I asked Tracy, 'What is the one thing you are learning from this?' She simply said, 'Let go and see your teenager fly.'

Action Points

1. Say hello to the coach.

As your child makes the transition to teenager, remember that this is your cue to change too. You need to learn a different way to communicate with her. She no longer requires you to manage her. You need to move on and define a new role for yourself. You need to become a coach to her. Make a list of what being a Parent Coach means to you and take action now.

2. Respect Board

Use a respect board in your house. It doesn't matter how you do it, just try it. Showing respect can be the key to unlocking good communication. Make it fun and make it up for everyone in the house, whether they participate or not. Don't put pressure on anyone, use it yourself but make it an option for everyone else.

3. Listen from her point of view.

Make it your sole purpose to truly listen to your teenager. Don't just hear what your teenager says while you are doing something else. Stop what you are doing, turn to face her when she speaks and really listen. Ask yourself how it must feel to be in her shoes, looking at things through her eyes, not yours. If you really want to challenge yourself for the next week keep your lips shut when you are with your teenager. Other than what is absolutely necessary don't say anything and see what happens. If all else fails, write the word WAIT somewhere where you can see it – **W**hy **A**m **I T**alking?

4. Clear communication

Look at your relationship with your teenager. Where could you give more responsibility and choice? Where could you let go a little more? Where do you need to be clearer in your communication, language and expectations? Allow her to prove to you that she can be responsible. When you hand responsibility to her, ensure that you make these points clear:

- What you are making her responsible for and why
- What you expect from her
- What will happen if she proves to be irresponsible
- Put a time limit on it
- Check that she understands.

For example:

'. . . I am handing responsibility for your bedtime over to you because I think you are old enough to make your own decisions about what time you go to bed. However, I expect that you will get yourself up for school on time each morning, refreshed and feeling alert. I also expect that you do not keep the rest of the house awake in the evenings. If you keep us awake or do not get up for school or do not appear refreshed and alert, I will take responsibility for fixing bedtime back for a month. Do you understand?'

When she proves to be responsible for one thing, then add more. Show her the reward for proving she can be responsible by giving her more freedom and independence about other things in her life.

5. Define the conditions of adulthood.

Be clear within your own mind about how you, as the parent, are setting an example for your teenager. How are you, by your actions, defining adulthood to your teenager? What are you teaching her about communication? What do you want your teenager to believe are the conditions of adulthood and how are you going to teach them to her? How can you improve yourself and so improve your teenager's view of adulthood? How can you start to teach your teenager what it takes to be an adult? Be clear yourself first, then devise a plan for how you are going to accomplish this.

6. Treat her like an individual.

If you want effective communication with your teenager then treat her like an individual. This is a tall order, I know. We do not have children just to fulfil our dreams, or for them to be exactly like us. We love their individuality and we are happy when we recognize part of ourselves in them. Have the courage to trust them; get out of their way and encourage them to live their lives in the way you have shown them.

5

My teenager will not stop fighting with her brother

It is constant and over every petty thing you can imagine, down to how much facial wash he has used. It is exhausting!

In this chapter I give you some suggestions on how to deal with sibling rivalry in your home. Sibling rivalry is something that any parent with more than one child will be used to. I think we have to accept that while people live in such close proximity to each other, at difficult times in their lives, they are bound to argue.

The point of this chapter is not to help your children behave like angels, it is to help them to deal with the outbursts themselves and come to their own conclusions about what is right and wrong. After all, life is full of disagreements and what we want is that they should learn how to deal with them themselves.

We will follow Kerri's and Steven's journey as they try to tame their terrible duo, Lexie and Jamie.

Case Study: Kerri and Steven, Lexie and Jamie

Kerri and Steven came to me about their 'little darlings', Lexie and Jamie. Lexie, fifteen, and Jamie, thirteen, were at each other's throats and it was world war three! They argued about everything from 'You pinched my CD' to who sat in the front of the car, to how much shower gel and facial wash one of them had used over the other. It was ridiculous and all the attempts that Kerri and Steven made were to no avail, the siblings still fought like cat and dog.

Kerri and Steven needed help and they needed it quickly. When dealing with sibling rivalry the worst thing you can do as a parent is to get involved. You need to find ways that allow you to take a back seat and encourage your children to take responsibility for their own actions. After all, when they go out into the big wide world you will not be there to sort out their differences, will you?

I initially met them at their home and they were at their wits' end. Kerri regularly had to call Steven home from work as the fighting had become so aggressive that she could not split the children up. Only recently they had had to take Jamie to hospital as Lexie had hit him with the phone and split his head open. Looking at their house, you would never have guessed what was going on inside it. The children had everything they could wish for: a beautiful home; private education; a house in Italy where they spent most holidays; and when they wanted something they just asked. It was hard to believe that they could be so violent. Kerri and Steven loved them both so much and as far as I could tell they did not favour one over the other. Their behaviour with their parents and in school was impeccable. The only difficulties really seemed to be the ones they had with each other.

I asked what would normally happen when they got into an argument and they told me how it would start over something little, like coming into a room without knocking, and this would escalate. One of them would come down and 'tell tales' on the other, then the other would come down and do the same. Then they would shout at each other while Kerri and Steven tried to appease them, not taking sides and not shouting. The whole thing would get worse and worse, and then someone would get hurt. Kerri and Steven were getting so involved in the arguments that the children were not learning how to handle them themselves. When I asked them what they wanted they simply said they wanted them to stop fighting and get on together. Without a magic wand and some pixie dust a 'happy ever after' ending was not going to happen. When it comes to families there are no fairy tales. There was, after all, nothing I could do that would make these two agree. It was for the children to do it themselves. So we framed our coaching target – to help Lexie and Jamie to come to their own conclusions and to manage their own ways of dealing with each other. In this way they would take responsibility for solving their problems between themselves without Kerri and Steven having to step in all the time.

Most parents find all the shouting and name-calling difficult to deal with, stepping in too soon to stop their own pain rather than just leaving the children to get on with it and sort it out themselves. They will never learn to deal with things if the parents keep stepping in.

The piece of homework I gave the parents was that they were not to step in unless situations became violent and aggressive. They were simply to leave their children to it and not worry about the screaming and the shouting and what the neighbours would say. If it became aggressive they were to separate the children and leave them in their respective rooms. When the children came down to them they were simply to say, 'I want *you* to work out the best way of dealing with this.'

Kerri and Steven were attempting to break a habit of a lifetime which was going to take time. They had to let Lexie and Jamie work it out for themselves.

They did what I had told them and every time one of the children came down they were told to go and work it out for themselves. The arguments went on for longer and over more and more petty things. Lexie and Jamie now screamed at their parents because they would not help and I received many frantic phone calls in which I told them that all they had to do was to be patient. Then a strange thing happened one day. Lexie came home with a bottle of facial wash, showing it to her mum proudly – not a great achievement perhaps, but it was backed up with, 'I am sick of arguing over the facial wash so I bought my own.' It was a step forward indeed. Through being left alone, Lexie had found her own solution. Kerri and Steven could see a breakthrough, albeit small. They continued for a few weeks, having to separate the children only a few times. When they did have to, they went in, removed one of them quietly and calmly, put them in another room and sat with them until they had calmed down.

Helping your children work things out for themselves is important, but you can help them further and show them the way by putting simple strategies in place that will resolve what they argue about the most. To do this we look at what I call the flash points (the things that cause the most arguments in the house) and think to ourselves, 'What could I do to resolve this?' By thinking this way we make life a lot easier for ourselves and that is what I needed to do with Kerri and Steven. When thinking of how to work this out, give your children some responsibility too. Put a few solutions in place so they can get a feel for how it is done and then let them figure out the rest on their own.

I asked Lexie and Jamie to make a list of the things the teenagers argued about most.

Lexie and Jamie's flash points were:

1. Who sits where in the car
2. Going into each other's room
3. Where they sit at the dinner table
4. The facial wash, which had been resolved
5. Who uses the bathroom and when
6. Annoying each other in front of friends.

Kerri and Steven decided to tackle the car, the dinner table and the bathroom problems first. Their solutions were:

1. The car – on Mondays, Wednesdays and Fridays, Lexie is in the front and on the other days Jamie is in the front, except on Sundays

when neither child is. It was either this arrangement or no one goes in the front.

2. The dinner table – they switch seats during the week on alternate days and on Sunday the whole family switches seats. If they argue about it they eat their dinner away from the rest of the family in the other room.

3. The bathroom – they agree an arrangement between themselves about who uses the bathroom and when.

All very well, you may think, but are we not just pandering to their every whim, you may ask? No, we are teaching them how to negotiate with each other to reach a situation where they both get what they want. This is not a skill that is taught and your children may need to see you doing it a few times before they pick up how it works. Sorting out problems and coming to a compromise and a solution where both parties are happy is not a skill we are born with! You need to show them how it is done. Whatever strategies you adopt, as parents you must be clear together on the ones you are using and keep a united front, otherwise you will have the children playing one of you off against the other. Be sure that as the parents you communicate with each other.

Steven and Kerri were to tell the children what they had decided. The next time the children argued about one of the flash points we had identified, they would be given five minutes to agree their own solution or else the parents' solution would be implemented.

TIME OUT ···

When implementing any strategies it is vital that you follow through and this is where most parents trip up. If you have said that you will not move the car until they stop arguing then you have to be prepared to do that. A lot of parents give in because of the demands on their time. If you give in then you are wasting your time, because you will have to do the whole thing many times again. If you remain firm, no matter what, then the time you see as wasted now will save you time in the long run. After all, what could be more important than teaching your children about consequences and responsibility?

Sure enough it did not take long before Kerri had to implement the car rule – the next day, in fact. After giving them five minutes no solution had been reached, so she simply enforced her own. This did not go down well at all with Lexie who straightaway sat in the front seat and refused to move.

FREEZE: WHAT WOULD YOU HAVE DONE? ··········

Would you have shouted? Given in? Called your partner to sort it out? Or stood firm and sat in the car for two hours?

Kerri called me from the car in a panic, not sure what to do. My advice was to sit tight and tell Lexie that she was not driving home until she moved and let Jamie sit there. She had to forget about the million and one jobs she had to do and win this. It was so important, so they sat there for two hours. Steven called, wondering where his dinner was, the children both yelled and screamed, but Kerri stayed firm. It was only when Lexie's friend called and asked her where she was that Lexie sprang into life and moved to the back seat. Kerri had won this battle and the two of them did not argue about the car again. The dinner table rule was also a success, despite the fact that Jamie decided he quite liked sitting in the other room having dinner by himself. Not quite the desired result but they had given him a choice and he had made it. The bathroom idea did not go so well, with Lexie saying the only agreement she would make would be that she would be able to use the bathroom whenever she wanted. Jamie continued pestering her when she was in the bath. It was clear they needed some more help.

It is important that you help your children to come to their own conclusions about what is the best way forward. They need to learn that their behaviour is not necessarily getting them what they want. When they begin to see the link between the two they are more likely to take action. Even just separating them when they are fighting and simply asking them whether what they are doing will give them what they want, can be very powerful!

I went back to the house to spend some time with Lexie and Jamie and asked them one simple question, 'What is it you want?' They both produced a list.

Lexie's list read:

- Peace
- Space
- Respect
- Time to think
- To be left alone and not to be interrupted.

Jamie's list read:

- I want her to leave me alone
- Stop annoying me
- Treat me like I am human
- Let me get on with my own thing
- Be nice sometimes.

'What do you notice about the lists?' I asked, as I showed them to them together. Stunned silence and they both looked long and hard for a while ... 'Er, they are very similar,' said Jamie. 'We both really want the same things,' said Lexie. 'Then why, if you both want the same, are you arguing so much?' I asked. Neither of them had the answer, however you could tell their brains were working and the message was hitting home, just by the looks on their faces. So with me as referee, we drew up a list of agreements between them that suited them both.

They were:

1. When one of us is in our room with the door shut, the other does not come in without knocking first.
2. If one of us is doing homework downstairs, the other leaves them to get on with it unless they have something really important to ask.
3. When one of us has invited a friend to the house, the other does not annoy us and just lets us do what we want.

We then had to decide what would happen if they broke the agreement and, for that, I handed it over to them. Together they came up with a very strange system which involved downloading for phones and i-pod which I will not even try to go into. I then asked what they thought they needed in order to carry this through and they said they needed someone to help them decide when a rule was broken or not. They chose Steven, as he was a lawyer; I think they saw him as more impartial.

When a rule was broken they reminded each other of their agreement and called in Steven who, as a lawyer could, weighed up the argument impartially and gave his verdict. Mostly, they agreed with him. When they didn't, they phoned their grandmother for a second opinion. What became so evident is that it was Lexie who actually did most of the annoying and I think realizing this shocked her and she began to annoy Jamie less.

I told Kerri and Steven that when Lexie and Jamie argued they were just to remind them of the three agreements they had made and to ask that they come to a conclusion together about what could be done. The bathroom took them much longer, though, and when they finally came to a conclusion it involved putting a washbasin and mirror in Lexie's bedroom. They had agreed that Lexie used the bathroom most for getting ready and that Jamie merely wanted the bathroom for ablutions. Since she used the bathroom more it made sense for her to have the washbasin and mirror in her room.

Kerri and Steven had a choice in this and decided that the arrangement was satisfactory. However, if the arguments continued they would take the basin and mirror out and put them in their own room. I know this may not be what you would want to do but it made them happy. The bathroom arguments stopped and all in all things were much better until one night. Lexie had called Jamie a swot and he in return had called her thick and stupid. All hell broke loose, and a few prize objets d'art were smashed. What was clear was that although the arguments had stopped and they were living together much better, they were still barely tolerating each other. What I had to get them to do was to understand each other and manage their emotions better.

To help them understand each other and work more as a family team I introduced them to a tool I like to use which is called the enneagram.

The enneagram identifies nine main personality types. While we each possess more than one of the nine types, we show preference to one more than the others. I find this tool extremely useful in helping teenagers to understand themselves and other people.

The Nine Personality Types

Type One – The Perfectionist

These are people who want everything to be perfect and will try really hard to get it right.

Type Two – The Helper

These people want to help in any way they can and sometimes at their own expense.

Type Three – The Achiever

These people just get on and do things, they achieve much and are successful in most things.

Type Four – The Romantic

These are the drama queens and are highly emotional, quite often playing out their own mini-tragedy.

Type Five – The Observer

These are objective people who sit back and watch, taking everything in and speaking only when necessary.

Type Six – The Questioner

As it suggests, these people ask questions, a lot of them, mostly of themselves, making it impossible to arrive at decisions.

Type Seven – The Adventurer

These people are born to have fun and to try out new experiences.

Type Eight – The Challenger

As the name says, these people challenge and assert their authority at every given minute.

Type Nine – The Peacemaker

These people are always trying to keep the peace and live in a little fantasy world, despite what is happening on the outside.

Each of the types has a way in which they see the world, a way in which they act in relationships and a gift they bring to the rest of us. Understanding our own personality types and those of other people can be of great help to us.

Lexie and Jamie enjoyed this process and what we discovered was that Jamie was a type one and Lexie a type seven. So we had a perfectionist who always wanted to do well and get it right teamed with an adventurer whose only motive was to have fun and try new things – and really if they made a mistake it was a bonus since they still learned something new. While on the surface this may have seemed like a match doomed from the beginning, there were some plus points here for them both to see. Lexie had the ability, if she used it, to help Jamie 'lighten up' a bit and start to have more fun. Jamie had the ability to support Lexie in finishing things and taking a little more care.

As the days went by the two of them began to understand each other more and Lexie even began to take some of her homework to her 'swot' brother to help her. He was able to support Lexie in making it more 'perfect' and her grades went up as a result. Lexie often told Jamie to 'lighten up' and even dared him a few times not to hand in homework which, as you can imagine, left Kerri and Steven with some tough talking to do with Lexie. Finally, they were able to appreciate what they could do for each other.

TIME OUT

We all get angry, it is a natural reaction. The only real problem comes when we cannot control this anger, adults and children alike. We all have a point at which we become uncontrollable and we 'snap'. This is something I call the boiling point. If we are pushed beyond this point we can no longer control our anger. For most teenagers this boiling point is very low. Before we reach the point of no control there will be things that we do or say that can be clues for the other person, indicating that it is time they left us alone. To stay around after this point would be foolish and would only make the situation worse. Supporting and helping a teenager to understand their own boiling points and communicate this to others can put an end to a lot of the 'blow-ups'.

I had Lexie and Jamie each describe to the other where their boiling points were. In understanding each other's boiling points they would know when they had pushed the other person too far and could walk away to prevent the situation from getting any worse. We discovered that Lexie sighed deeply before becoming really angry and losing control and Jamie would shout 'go away' before he was about to let rip. They both learned to walk away when they had these cues from each other. Steven and Kerri also helped by reminding them when they were taking the situations too far.

Armed with this information our squabbling duo were able to put their war weapons down and come to some sort of peace treaty. It had taken them four months, nothing was perfect and they still 'had their moments' as Kerri and Steven put it, but at least they could now be taken out in public. They have even, on the odd occasion, been fond of and rather pleasant to each other.

Action Points

1. Get out of their way.

This is their battle, let them fight it themselves. Let them sort out their arguments. Squabbling is all part of being human, and something our little darling aliens need to learn to deal with. Only step in if you can see or smell blood! Other than that, tell them you want them to go away and think about what they are doing, to decide what they want and then to agree their own solutions. After all, this is a lesson they need to learn.

2. Don't play them at their game.

Don't let them involve you in their games. Make it clear you will not take sides and step in. It is up to them to sort out their squabbling. Becoming involved in their arguments is the worst thing you can do!

3. Show them how it is done.

Remember, your little darlings are not quite the masters at putting solutions in place yet. Their minds are too busy thinking, 'How can I win this?' rather than 'How can I make sure everyone gets what they want?' Teenager aliens are out for themselves! Help them learn this skill by putting some solutions in place first so they can see how it is done. Take the top three things they argue about the most and find a solution for each that will suit both and is fair, then implement it. Remember to give them a choice: 'You either sit in the front on alternate days or no one sits in the front,' and be prepared to stick by what you have said! Think of Kerri in the car for two hours – that is what it may take.

4. Divide and conquer.

If things between your squabbling duo get too rough, separate them. Put one in one room and the other in another, asking them to think about what they want, what they are doing and if what they are doing will get them what they want.

5. Help them decide what it is they want.

They may decide they actually want the same thing.

6. Help them come to their own conclusions.

Don't step in, but ask them how they can come to agreements themselves about the important things.

7. Help them understand each other.

Help them to understand themselves and their siblings. This may enable them to deal with each other in different ways. Support them in understanding each other's boiling points.

8. Allow them to disagree.

Remember they are siblings and perfect peace may never be reached; accept for yourselves as parents that there may be times when they just don't get on.

6

My teenager so easily succumbs to peer pressure

How can I help him to resist peer pressure, be able to say no and walk away from unwise choices, situations and decisions?

The purpose of this chapter is to guide you through a process that you can use with your children that will help them in making wiser choices and decisions. All parents want to ensure that their children make good and wise choices, and when we can see them throwing their lives away it is heartbreaking.

I think we must be realistic in these situations and remember that this is not about the pursuit of perfection. All teenagers will do bad things, make bad choices and get into trouble. It is the way they learn what feels right and wrong for them. The question here is, do you have children who feel strong enough to make their own decisions and not to be influenced by what others are doing or want them to do? This will be the subject of this chapter.

We will follow Sharon's and Phil's journey as they try to tame their out-of-control son Danny.

Case Study: Sharon, Phil and Danny

....

Meet our frazzled parents, Sharon and Phil, and their difficult teenager, Danny. Danny is thirteen years old and a handful. When his parents came to see me Danny was on his final warning from the police for an assault. He was hanging around with a much older gang and spent most of his time smoking and drinking. He spent no time at home at all and when his parents grounded him he would just escape out of the bedroom window. He would swear and shout and call his mum all the names under the sun. He did not respect anyone and when asked about his behaviour he would just say he didn't care and he thought it was 'cool'. He would regularly brag about his conquests and all the things he got up to. Sharon and Phil had tried everything, including psychologists, and I really was their last resort.

When dealing with children like Danny we must not be overwhelmed by the situation. 'Petty' criminality is often habitual. In fact, a lot of behaviour is habit, resulting from choices we make over and over again in response to certain stimuli. Teenagers make choices and so do adults. Only when we can observe our own behaviour can we begin to make different choices. This is what makes coaching so useful. It makes us observe our own behaviour so that we can change the choices that are fuelling it. All this takes time and any lasting change takes between six and eighteen months. That is why coaching is a long-term investment. However, in extreme cases, the process can be speeded up by removing people from the situation that triggers the familiar patterns. When we remove a teenager from his familiar circle, we shock his system. This is one of the reasons why people often feel different on holiday. When you can, and where time is of the essence, it is always a good idea to break the pattern with a quick, hard shock. You can then implement a new strategy where everyone can see the situation afresh.

I took an unusual step and suggested to Danny and his parents that we should all go away for a week, together. From what Sharon and Phil had told me I felt that the most important thing we needed was to break the pattern. Most of the time, this can be done over a period of time and more gently. But in Danny's case we had only a month before he was due to appear before a Youth Offending Panel and his case was urgent. Sharon and Phil agreed to my suggestion.

So, a week later there we all were in a hotel in the Dales – five days and counting. Danny, I can tell you, was not happy. In fact if looks could kill I would not even be writing this. However, I was determined, armed with a plan and I intended to plough forward regardless. While we were away the plan was twofold: to spend the mornings with Danny coaching him and then the afternoons with the whole family (including eight-year-old Heidi) putting together a new way forward.

When we are thinking about badly behaved teenagers like Danny, we automatically think they alone are the problem and visions of boot camps automatically come to mind. However good these camps may be, what they cannot do is change the environment surrounding the child. If Danny alone changes and then goes back to his family who are still the same as they were before he left, he will soon revert to his old behaviour. Any intervention that deals with children like Danny must also acknowledge the behaviour of the parents and siblings, too. This was the reason my time was split between the family and him.

In my experience, teenagers who are 'acting up' as Danny was, are doing so because they have certain physical, mental and emotional needs that are not being met. My time with Danny had to focus on this and on finding out why he was doing what he was doing and what needs it was meeting for him. I then had to work on finding other ways to meet those needs. Only by getting to the root of the problem could any lasting change occur. This was not a job for a sticking plaster. Major surgery was needed and this was going to take time, patience and a lot of strength. As a parent dealing with this sort of child you must be realistic about what you can expect and get yourself ready for a long and arduous journey!

Day One for me was all about finding out why Danny did the things he did. Why were his friends so important and what did he get from being with them; what did he get from them that he did not get at home? I spoke to Danny for over an hour, attempting as hard as I could to find all this out. All I got from him was lots of huffs, grunts and a series of 'Dunnos'. Not getting anywhere, I decided to try a different approach.

Sharon and Phil had told me how much he liked to brag so I asked him about what he got up to and it all flooded out. He told me about what he did with his mates, and how they were feared on the estate. I listened carefully and attempted to see things from his point of view. I found that Danny saw it all as exciting and challenging. It gave him a sense of competitiveness and status, of being the best. I asked him how it felt when he was doing all these things. That was it, he opened up and his eyes began to gleam. 'I just get such a buzz, I feel as if I am invincible, I feel as if I am good at something and that I am okay.' Bingo! Now I was getting somewhere. So while on a roll I asked Danny how he felt when he was at home. 'Well, I just feel bored mainly and that I am no good at anything. I feel trapped and I want to get out.' I now had something to work on. If we could make Danny feel the same way at home as he did with his friends, then he would be likely to spend more time at home.

'All well and good,' you may say, 'but how do we apply this to our home?' You wait for your teenagers to talk to you and then you listen. Don't judge what they are saying and don't butt in, just listen. Let them talk and tell you what they do with their friends; let them be open. Listen, so that you can understand their point of view, and think how it feels to be your son or daughter. Does being with their friends make them feel grown up and excited? If they say it is exciting, then ask what you could all do together at home that would be as exciting. If they say it makes them feel grown up, ask how you can make them feel more grown up. Don't expect an answer straight away and don't expect them to jump with excitement. Two things I have definitely learnt by being with teenagers are that when you think what you are saying is being absorbed, it probably is not – and when you think you are getting nowhere, they are probably taking it in and understanding it!

So back to Danny. After three hours with him and with lots of persistence I had learnt that Danny's primary objectives were:

1. To have fun and excitement
2. To face challenges and take risks
3. To be in charge and feel important
4. To win and feel the best
5. To be free.

The next step was to get the whole family together round the table. We had five sheets of flipchart paper. At the top of each piece of paper was written one of Danny's five objectives. For the fun and excitement sheet I asked Danny to describe to the rest of the family what these words meant to him and then each family member did the same. They then wrote on the paper a list of ten things that were fun and exciting to them *as a family*. We did the same with each of the other objectives. Everyone learnt a good deal during the process. Sharon thought fun was watching a video together or doing something inside the house. Danny only thought things outside the house were fun. Phil was scared of risk and disagreed with most of what Danny wrote because of his own fear. Sharon and Danny both liked control and fought for this. It was an enlightening conversation. At the end of this session, we found, for the time being, one thing that they could do in each area that would encourage Danny to spend more time at home. Here is what they agreed:

1. Once a month they would all spend a day doing something *exciting and fun*.
2. Every few months they would participate in some kind of extreme sport so that they might face *challenges and risks*.

99

3. Danny was to *be in charge* of allocating the household budget (mad, I know! – that is what I thought, too). This was his suggestion and he was to be closely monitored for the first six months by Phil.
4. Danny was going to take up rugby to help him *feel the best and win*.
5. On their camping weekends away they agreed to buy a new tent for Danny *to be free* and stay in by himself, or take a friend if he wished.

It is important to note that Danny was asked for his suggestions and they could only be included if the rest of the family agreed. There were some clauses; for instance, that Sharon and Heidi could opt out of if they wished, such as the extreme sport. You may not be so lucky in being able to get your teenager round the table to discuss such things. What I recommend you do then is, after you have found out what is important to him, hazard a guess at what may appeal to him and make a suggestion like, 'Danny, we are thinking of buying you a separate tent when we go on holiday so you can be freer to do what you want and are able to bring a friend if you like – what do you think?' You will know by his reaction if you are on course. If you get nowhere then just ask what he would suggest.

Day Two saw a different Danny. He appeared a little happier and a little more open. It was time for me to find out what he thought about himself. I gave him a big piece of paper and some spray cans, asked him to create something that expressed to me who he was and left him alone for an hour. When I went back I was shocked. He had written the words 'Gangs', 'Drugs', 'Alcohol', 'Designer Labels' and 'Escaping the Police' in large letters. Danny had only identified himself with things that were outside him, not qualities, not things inside, and they were all negative. I tried in vain to show him the difference between who he was inside and who he was outside. So I then asked him to show me. He quickly decided that he should walk with me round the local town so he could show the town who was boss.

Teenagers are bombarded with negative opinions of themselves daily, from the media, their school or from you. It is sometimes not surprising that they feel so bad about themselves. It becomes hard for them to associate with anything other than what they have been told. They begin to identify with the traits which others judge them to have, and these eventually become part of their personality. However, it is quite easy to change this. Instead of disapproving of all they do and all they appear to be, it only requires you to become curious. Start searching for what is good about them, start to use the negatives as positives. Let me show you an example.

Rather than comment on his attitude, I just agreed and off we went together, me lagging behind as Danny did his showing off. All the while I asked him questions and made comments, so when he looked at the designer labels I said, 'So you take pride in your appearance?' When he talked to me about the things he and his gang did I said, 'So it is important that you socialize with other people you like?' For everything he said and did I replied with a positive quality about him. After an hour we went back. I produced a big white board and began to write a list of all the things we had discovered about Danny: he was sociable; he cared how he looked; he liked being with other people; he liked excitement and feeling important; he wanted to win, and so on. We numbered them on the board and soon reached ten. Danny suddenly became very interested and took the board from me, telling me how he was proficient at putting things together, was good with animals, cared for his sister and was daring. The list grew.

When we were back together with Sharon and Phil I left it to Danny, who showed them the list and excitedly went through it with them. He claimed he had learnt that he was really good at some things and he was not all bad, that he would rather strip a car engine than get into trouble with the police. He was a different person and what they had as a family now was a list showing how they could motivate Danny and make him feel better about himself.

When we think of raising a teenager's self-esteem and self-respect we think of it as a long and difficult job, but really it can be as quick and simple as it was with Danny. When your teenager does something, whatever it is, show him what is good about himself, what quality you see in him. If he continues asking to go out when you have said no, understand and acknowledge his persistence. When he complains about how unfair something is, recognize and acknowledge his need for justice. When you continue to do this daily, his opinion of himself will change. If you want to go one step further, write the good qualities down on a board. I can almost guarantee that at first your teenager will stick his nose up at the idea. But believe me, there is something powerful about seeing these things written down. Secretly he will love it.

Day Three, and Danny was waiting for me in the lobby of the hotel with his white board in hand. For about thirty minutes he read to me all the things that were good about him. I was delighted, something in his face had softened and he was full of energy. It was time to move on. I let Danny know that today we had one mission and that was to create the Danny Party, like the Labour Party only different! We were going to create a manifesto for his life, what he stood for. He, as you can imagine, looked at me very blankly.

Teenagers often go along with their friends and make unwise choices and decisions because they don't really know what is important to them. Consequently, it is not easy for them to make good judgements. Helping teenagers to discover their core values in life provides a good base for them to work from and can be the most important piece of work you do.

For the next few hours I asked Danny many questions and asked him to describe to me things that made him mad, happy, annoyed and sad. I asked him to talk about people he admired, to describe times in his life when he felt on top of the world. I was attempting to get out of Danny what was important to him. Eventually we established five things to put in his manifesto.

1. **Fairness** – Danny actually had a real sense of justice and did not agree with bigger people picking on smaller people.
2. **Being the best** – he loved feeling that he was the best at something and felt dejected when he was not at the top.
3. **Being outspoken** – he believed he should speak his mind.
4. **Listening** – he hated not being listened to.
5. **Honesty** – Danny did not like it when people lied to him or were dishonest.

We were getting somewhere so I then asked Danny to write a few sentences to describe each item. For example, for fairness he wrote:

'I think everyone deserves a chance and that we should treat everyone the same.' After he had done this we looked at what he needed to do to be true to himself – if fairness was important to him, who was he treating unfairly and how could he change that? This was a truly lengthy process and all we really had time for at the end of the day was to show it to the rest of the family. They had to hold him to it. We decided that when they returned home it would be pinned up in his bedroom and in the kitchen.

TIME OUT

So how do you use this at home? You don't have to do it as openly as I did if you have a teenager who will not work with you – you can sneak this under the radar, so to speak. You can of course just ask the question, 'What is important to you?' Alternatively, when they are happy, sad, angry or excited, find out what makes them angry. Is it not being listened to, or being treated unfairly? Try to make them aware of the underlying reason. Then, in turn, when they are not listening to you, remind them of how important it was for them, and how angry they were when nobody listened to them, and how they are now doing the same to you. It will take more time but it will be effective.

Now that Danny was changing and learning what was important to him, it was time for Sharon and Phil to start looking at how they were treating Danny and what they could do differently. As he changed and began to transform, so they needed to also.

As I spoke to Sharon and Phil it became obvious that they needed to take responsibility for their part in the problem. They were so worried that he would make the wrong decision that as he continued to go more off the rails they continued to trust him less. This was understandable and their lack of trust meant that they were stepping in to 'save' him sometimes before they needed to. They were assuming every decision he made was going to be a 'bad' one. They needed to allow him to make decisions and not be afraid that he would make the wrong ones. They needed to learn to trust him again.

Phil and Sharon could now see that their lack of trust had led them to try and control Danny rather than to understand him.

Day Four, and it felt as if it was time finally to tackle the peer pressure and its effects on Danny. We had done the groundwork, he now knew what he stood for, and it was therefore easier to make decisions.

We took a typical situation where Danny felt he would be pressurized into doing something. He chose smoking dope, which apparently he did not even like but just did it because everyone else did. We looked at his manifesto and I asked which one of the five points does this choice relate to? He quickly answered, 'Being the best – if I smoke then my mind is not sharp and I cannot do and be my best and I could get caught.' We went through a variety of different situations from doing well at school to breaking the rules at home and for each one we applied the same test. Danny could clearly see that a lot of the choices he was making were not the choices he wanted. He needed help to deal with this.

I suggested that in any future situation when he found himself under pressure to do something he didn't like, he should quickly ask himself whether it fitted in with what he wanted to do; whether it was in his manifesto. If it did not fit then he should let the others know, clearly and firmly, what he had decided to do. After that, he should let any further persuasion or taunts roll over him like water off a duck's back. Learn to 'be a duck', in effect.

Danny now felt he was much better able to deal with his friends, whatever they said to him. He knew that he could now pick how he thought about what people said to him. This gave him power as well as strength in his own conviction. That day, after discussing together as a family what they had learnt and what was the way forward, they left to go home. They had all the tools they needed and it was up to them to use them in the home environment. It was up to Sharon and Phil to motivate Danny and encourage him to stick up for what he believed in. It was up to them to remember to let him make his own mistakes and still encourage and support him in the positives. Most important of all, it was up to Danny to take control of his life and himself.

When he appeared before the Youth Offending Panel Danny was given community service, which was really good going considering his offence. Sharon believed this was partly due to the fact that he told the panel all he had learnt. She and Phil began to implement what they had learnt and things began to improve. It has been over two years since I spent those few days with Sharon, Phil and Danny and Heidi. They are well and truly on the road to a better life together. Danny, now fifteen, has not been in trouble since and has a completely different set of friends. The situation in the home has improved tenfold and the family do things together. Sharon and Phil have a better relationship with Danny and in the turbulent teenage years that is a great achievement in itself.

Action Points

. . . .

1. Break the cycle.

If you want to make progress with your teenager, consider how you can break the cycle of everyday life and help him to do different things. A holiday is ideal, although it may not be possible to go right away, as I did with Danny and his family. The important thing is to make a change away from the familiar, to somewhere fresh or to an activity that you know he enjoys. Change the environment or surroundings and you may start to change the way he thinks and reacts.

2. What is driving him?

If you want to become influential in your teenager's life then make it your job to discover what his objectives are. After all, you know him the best and you should be the one able to work this out. Ask what is important to him and make a list. When he shares things with you, ask how he feels. If something is on the news, ask what he thinks about it. Make this a three-month project to discover what your teenager is concerned about. When he comes in after being with his friends, show an interest in what he did and find out why he enjoyed it. He may not speak to you at first, but when he realizes that you are not criticizing him he will begin to speak more.

3. Make home the place to be.

When you know what is driving your teenager, look at ways that you can bring more of what he does outside the home to inside it. Ask him what would make him want to spend more time with you. Consider your teenager's views and what he wants when you are planning things as a family. Don't just assume that what appears to be his lack of interest means he is not interested. The more of a relationship you can build and the more time you can spend with him, the more influence you can have.

4. The Teenager Manifesto

Take on the task of understanding your teenager. Help him to understand that he is strong and can make his own decisions. Take everything he says to you as being on the surface and make it your job to dig a little deeper. If he is happy, find out why; if he is angry, find out why. Really find out about what he does, what he believes in and what motivates him. If he will prepare his own 'manifesto' all well and good, but you may have to help. Eventually, you need to establish the things that are most important to your teenager.

5. Help him to see the difference between right and wrong.

When your teenager is making choices or decisions, support him by referring back to his manifesto or the things that you have identified as important to him. By doing this you will be helping him to use this skill when he is with his peers and has to make decisions.

6. Build him up.

Make a decision to build your teenager up, not knock him down. By doing this you will be helping him to feel better about himself, to gain more confidence and in turn to be better able to stick up for himself.

7. Trust him.

One of the biggest gifts you can give him is your trust. You have no idea how much this means to him. When he is making decisions, let him know you trust him to come to the right decision and you will support him if he needs it. Show him in small ways every day that you trust him and in return you will get more trustworthy behaviour.

7

My teenager is my step-child

I am not sure where I fit into her life. Should I be her friend, parent or something else? Her father just thinks I'm being paranoid but I am sure she does not like me.

Being a step-parent to a teenager is extremely difficult and my heart goes out to all of you who are reading this. The relationship between teenager and step-parent is a fine and delicate balance, one that must be maintained and nurtured at all times. This chapter aims to guide step-parents through those teenage years.

It does not have to be a painful experience and with a little forethought, some planning and a lot of patience you can make the situation better.

We will follow Karen's journey as she attempts to mend the broken relationship with her step-daughter Lauren.

Case Study: Karen and Lauren

When Karen came to me she was frantic. She was sure that her sixteen-year-old step-daughter, Lauren, hated her. Lauren made Karen's life a nightmare from the minute she got up to the minute she went to bed. She ignored her, shouted at her, was rude to her, swore at her, played loud music when Karen was trying to work and would bring friends over when Karen had said not to. Karen was regularly subjected to the 'you are not my mother' jibe and Karen's husband Neil did nothing about it. He always appeared to side with Lauren, saying it must be difficult for her and that Karen needed to be more understanding. Karen felt unwanted and uncomfortable in her own home. She had been married to Neil for a year and the problems had really been going on from the beginning. Lauren had refused to go to the wedding. She would regularly phone her mum in Karen's presence and talk about her. Karen's relationship with Neil was in a critical state and if the situation did not improve there was every possibility that they would split up. I was not only helping to save a teenager here, I was also helping to save a marriage.

This situation is quite common and in essence is the result of Karen and Neil not being clear, before they were married, what would and would not be acceptable in the house. It is very difficult to integrate everybody into a new family. To expect them all to get along and live happily ever after may be one step too far. Further, to go ahead and ignore that issues may exist is foolhardy. Karen and Neil could have made this situation better by discussing beforehand any thoughts and feelings everyone might have had and by putting some structure in place that would meet the needs of all involved. By not making firm agreements with each other about what was acceptable behaviour from Lauren, they were putting their own relationship in jeopardy as well as the relationship between Lauren and Karen.

When Karen came to see me she was very angry and frustrated. It was obvious to me that before we could make any progress we had to deal with the feelings that Karen had about these relationships. The first thing I said to Karen was, 'Tell me how all this makes you feel.' Karen exploded into a tirade of emotions: 'I feel useless'; 'like no one cares'; 'like I am a bad person'. It went on for over thirty minutes.

Sometimes as parents we try to deny our feelings, thinking that perhaps they will go away or that the child is more important than we are. It is important that we acknowledge how and what we feel because harbouring feelings will only make us resent our child. We all tell ourselves powerful negative stories about how bad we are, how dreadful the situation is and how our life is in ruins. We are actually all quite the little scriptwriters of our own tragedies. These stories have great power over us and we need to bring them out in the open, to name and shame them and to see how ridiculous they really are. The ability to move forward comes when we acknowledge where we are right now, however good or bad, and how we feel about it. Then, and only then, can we begin to face the truth of the situation.

After Karen had finished her rant she looked at me and said, 'Gosh, I feel so much better,' and I could see that she did. She had finally admitted what she had been dying to say to someone for over a year. She had finally faced up to reality. I sent Karen away and gave her an assignment, which was to write down her story, the things she was telling herself, and read it every day. Needless to say, she did not feel happy about this but she was willing to try it.

Karen came back with a smile on her face. 'Wow, you look happy,' I said. 'Yes,' she said. 'I have realized two things. One is that the story I am telling myself is ridiculous. I cannot believe that I have been holding on to it for so long. The second is that this really is not about Lauren at all, it is about me and how I am handling myself with her.' I was delighted. I would normally have expected this type of revelation after months, not a week. This showed that Karen and I could make some significant strides forward.

When we face our parenting gremlins, those little voices which tell us we are no good, we give them less power. The more we actually listen to them and hear what they have to say, the more we realize that they are wrong and, as Karen said, ridiculous. When you are feeling out of control and emotional in any situation, the best thing to do is to deal with the facts of the situation first. The facts are things that we have control over and can change – for example, you may be tired and need to go to bed earlier. When we deal with the facts first, the feelings we have about the situation seem to get easier and we begin to feel stronger and better able to deal with the situation.

Karen and I then took a big piece of paper and put a line down the middle. On one side of the line I wrote the heading 'facts' and on the other side I wrote 'feelings'. On the feelings side, Karen and I wrote all the feelings that she had about the situation such as anger, helplessness, abandonment, frustration. On the other side we listed the facts, including: 'Lauren will not speak with me'; 'Lauren and I do not have a relationship'; 'Lauren's dad does not back me up'; – just the facts, not how she felt about them. I then said to Karen, 'So here is the situation in front of you, what do you want to work on first, the facts or the feelings?' I knew which she would choose but I had to ask anyway. 'The facts,' she said, 'without any shadow of doubt.'

Karen and I now had a plan. She was going to work on the facts of the situation so we picked her top three.

1. Lauren's dad does not back me up.
2. Lauren and I do not have a relationship.
3. I am not comfortable in my own home.

It was evident from most of Karen's list that to make any headway she and Neil needed to work more as a team. Parenting as a team is crucial and never more so than when you are in a house with a 'blended family'. Teamwork is as important in the home as it is in any large corporation. You need to show a united front towards your children. They need to know that there is consistency and continuity between you. When this is not evident a child becomes confused and begins to be manipulative, playing one parent off against the other. The first thing we needed to do was get Karen and Neil thinking like a team and coming to agreements about how they were going to parent Lauren.

So far, Neil and Karen had no agreements on this, no boundaries at all about what was and was not all right in the house and therefore Lauren did as she liked. So the first thing was for them to be clear about what they wanted as parents. I asked each of them to write a list of ten things that were important for them as parents and then to select from their lists ten points *on which they both agreed*. It took them three weeks to do this, which said a lot about their stormy relationship. Their agreed list was as follows:

1. Everyone in the house is to respect the others, their space and needs.
2. Everyone in the house is to be civil to the others, no swearing or shouting.
3. It is Lauren's responsibility to get to college on time.
4. One meal will be eaten together every day.
5. Friends are only invited over if all family members agree, except for unexpected visits.
6. We support each other in all endeavours.
7. Each month we have a family day out that is fun.
8. Lifts will only be provided if suitable to all parties and if advance notice is given.
9. All jobs within the house are to be shared equally.
10. Everyone in the house is to be responsible for managing his or her own money.

I did have to change it slightly for them. When I first saw it every point said, 'Lauren must do this, Lauren must do that . . .' which I changed into 'everyone' where appropriate.

Now that they had their parenting agreement the next step was to show this to Lauren. They had to present it as a team. They had to ensure that Lauren knew that she could ask any questions or make changes after consultation but she had to be aware that the conditions applied from this time forward.

To say that this did not go well would be an understatement. Neil and Karen had decided to approach Lauren and ask her to sit down with them at the family table as they wanted to discuss some new agreements. She said something to the effect that, 'If you think I am sitting down with that "bleep bleep" you have another think coming.' Karen ran off in tears and Neil sat there like a 'wet blanket', to use Karen's words. As you can imagine they were distraught when they next came to see me. All was not lost. I told them to go home and place the list in a prominent place and just calmly tell Lauren where it was. They did this and there was no reaction from Lauren whatsoever. If anything, she became worse. A full-scale row developed between Karen and Lauren which ended with Lauren saying she would do anything to split up her and Neil.

FREEZE: WHAT WOULD YOU HAVE DONE? ·········
Would you have slapped her? Walked out? Rung Neil up in
tears? Given up on the relationship as a bad job? Or would
you have asked Neil to get his superman costume on and take
some action?

It was time for drastic action. Neil needed to 'step up to the plate' and
show us what he was made of.

Neil needed to get much tougher with Lauren. He was allowing
her to undermine Karen and by not stepping in he was allowing her
to think it was okay. Some parents can let the guilt they feel get in
the way and they make excuses for a child's behaviour. This means
that the child gets away with things that ordinarily would not be
acceptable. Do not make excuses for your child, the situation may
be difficult and your daughter has feelings but that does not mean
that she can behave so abominably. Understanding your teenager's
point of view is a great thing and acknowledging what she feels is
admirable, but don't let this stop her learning common decency!

Neil had to let Lauren know that she must not speak to Karen as she did,
so I gave him a four-step system to follow every time that Lauren said
something to Karen that was unacceptable.

1. **State the behaviour that is unacceptable.**
   'Lauren, do you know that you are being unkind to Karen?'

2. **Tell her that it is not okay.**

   'Lauren, it is not acceptable for you to be unkind to Karen. She is my wife and I love her very much.'

3. **Let her know how it makes you feel.**

   'When you are unkind to Karen it makes me think that you do not care about me, what I feel and what is important to me.'

4. **Tell her the consequences if she continues.**

   'If you continue to do this then I will become unhappy, more stressed and will therefore be less patient and a misery to be with.'

Notice how we are only stating how it made Neil feel. The list does not touch on how it made Karen feel. There are two reasons for that: one, we can assume that Lauren does not care how Karen feels at the moment; and two, Neil can only speak for himself.

Neil was really unsure of this at first but loved Karen and was willing to do it for her. So that night when he came home he had a long conversation with Lauren following the system we had set up. She did not say much apparently, but she did apologize, and she cried. From then on, when Lauren was swearing and shouting at Karen, she simply said, 'Lauren, do you realize you are swearing and shouting at me? It is not acceptable for you to do that.' The first time she said it Lauren stormed off saying she did not care, but as time went on she began to apologize and then stopped swearing altogether in front of Karen.

For a few months all Neil and Karen did was use this approach. One afternoon I had an excited email from Karen saying that Lauren had asked her if she could go through the list of agreements with her and Neil that night. I gave her some advice – to let Lauren have a say, ask her what she thinks of each item and how she thinks they can achieve this as a family. They did exactly as I said and Lauren came up with some good ideas. She set her own bedtime. She told Neil and Karen how difficult she found it when they were being all 'lovey-dovey' in her presence and asked that they respect her space and feelings when they were around. She even suggested ways that the family could all have fun together. She asked to be put in charge of making up a duties roster (perhaps so she could have the pick of the best jobs) and asked Neil to go through some financial arrangements with her. As a family they came to an agreement about what each one of the agreed rules meant and what the consequences of breaking them would be. If Lauren did not give enough notice she would not get a lift; if she invited friends round without asking she would not be allowed to have them round for two weeks, and so on. Things in the home were definitely calmer and more pleasant and Karen did not feel constantly under attack. However, she and Lauren still had no kind of relationship. This was the next thing for us to deal with, bringing us back to the second point in the plan Karen and I had drawn up earlier.

Karen and I both knew that this was a delicate situation and the mere fact of Karen saying that she wanted a relationship with Lauren would not make it magically happen. Step-relationships are very delicate and must be handled with care. To me this needed a soft approach, something that would make Karen feel in control and would not make Lauren feel threatened. I decided to tell Karen about the 'listen and respect' technique.

TIME OUT ···

Listen and Respect is an easy technique to implement and the result can be very successful when used over long periods of time.

1. When your teenager talks just listen; close your mouth and listen.
2. While you are listening ask yourself, 'What is good about this person?' 'What do I really admire in her?'
3. When there is an opportune moment, tell her the answer you came up with. 'I really respect your determination,' 'I really admire your persistence,' 'What I think is good about you is your sense of humour.'

Don't make a big song and dance about it, just let her know what you find good about her at that time.

···

When I told Karen about this she initially told me that I had gone mad and I was 'having a laugh'. I assured her that it was what was needed in these circumstances. All she had to do was to use this technique on the few occasions that Lauren made an attempt to speak with her. Karen again did what I suggested. It was difficult at first because Lauren said so little to her. However, she tried it for a whole month and did notice that Lauren appeared to be talking to her more.

Then came the turning point, the day when Lauren reached out to Karen as she never had before. Lauren came home from college as usual and rather than going straight up to her room she hung around in the front room. It was obvious there was something wrong. Karen really wanted her to know that she was there to support her so she just said, 'Hi Lauren, is there anything I can help you with?' Lauren just looked at her and said, 'Well, something happened at college today that I wanted to talk to dad about. Can I talk to you instead?' Karen, as you can imagine, had to contain her excitement and calmly said, 'Yes.' Lauren and Karen talked for two hours that day and Neil came home to find them both laughing and talking together in the kitchen making dinner. He too had to contain himself. As the days went on Karen and Lauren spoke more and their relationship blossomed. Of course it had its ups and downs like any relationship and it was not always plain sailing.

Now that the relationship between Karen and Lauren was better, Karen was finding it increasingly difficult to ask for what she wanted. She did not want to damage the relationship in any way and was sacrificing some of the things she wanted in order to improve it.

Like most step-parents she was not sure where she fitted in – friend, parent or what? Although you have parental responsibilities, acting as a true parent may not be the best way to have a relationship with a teenager. To be a friend is also out of the question because that is not your job. How can you have parental responsibility and at the same time provide friendly support? Stop thinking about what your individual job is and start thinking as a team. Your job is to be a team player, part of a team of people all dedicated to each other. That way you can take the pressure off yourself and start as you mean to go on.

As part of a team Karen had as much right as the other team members to ask for what she wanted. In fact, if she didn't she could jeopardise the whole team due to her resentment.

It was time to begin work on her third stage, which was to feel more comfortable in her own home. So I asked Karen, 'What would make you feel more comfortable in your house at the moment?' She was very quick to answer.

1. Having my own friends round – friends that I had before I met Neil and Lauren.
2. Bringing some of my belongings out of storage and putting them in the house.
3. Putting some of my own photos up in the house.
4. Being involved in financial decisions that involve Lauren.
5. Being able to say 'no' to Lauren and having it accepted by Neil.

This seemed fair enough to me. We discussed how she wanted to do all this. She wanted it to be low-key and acceptable to both Neil and Lauren. She decided simply to ask, to make a request and see what happened. This is how we worded it: 'I have a request to make. I would really like to be able to invite friends round occasionally, to move some of my furniture into the house and to put up some of my photos so that I can feel more comfortable. I know that this house is not just mine so I want to know how you feel about this.' We decided to start with the first three, which were the easiest, and to her surprise they were accepted with no struggle. Karen moved in some of her belongings and her photos and started inviting her friends round. She checked what she needed to do to make Neil and Lauren feel comfortable with it so she did not overstep the mark and everything went well. When it came to items four and five she needed longer discussions with Neil that took weeks, but eventually they came to agreements about how this would be done. For example, saying 'no' to Lauren was all right as long as it was discussed with Neil first.

Eighteen months after I first met Neil and Karen things are unrecognizable. Karen and Lauren have a special relationship that is not friends, not parent and step-daughter, but something else. They still fall out and Karen and Neil sometimes do not always get things right. However, Karen is feeling so much more comfortable in the house and the three of them have become a family. They are a team of people who work together to make sure everyone gets what they want.

Action Points

1. Tame those parenting gremlins.

Get those gremlins out in the open, and as a step-parent you may have many! What are you telling yourself? Meet those gremlins head on and acknowledge them. Write out your whole story and read it every day for a week.

2. Facts and feelings

When your step-alien appears to be winning the battle, take control of the situation and start to take charge. Find a different perspective, an objective view of the situation. Divide a piece of paper into two; on one side write the facts and on the other write your feelings. Now make a decision to begin to deal with the facts one by one, the smallest first.

3. Parenting agreements

Sit down with your partner and make a list of what is important to both of you, how you are going to act as parents together, and how you are going to deal with your teenager. Make sure that you are both heading in the same direction. Discuss your list with your teenager and ask for her cooperation. Discuss what each item requires and what any consequences will be.

4. Four-Step System

Just as Neil did, start using the Four-Step System to let your teenager know what is unacceptable to you.

1. State the behaviour that is unacceptable.
2. Let her know that this is not okay.
3. Let her know how it makes you feel.
4. Tell her the consequences if she continues.

5. Listen and Respect

Just as Karen did, start using the Listen and Respect technique whenever you get the chance.

6. Ask for what you want.

Yes, you are allowed to make a list of what you want and begin to ask for it. Acknowledge that you have a place in the house too, even though others may feel slightly uncomfortable with you. Tread carefully, ask others what they need.

7. Teamwork

Stop thinking of yourself and your step-child as opponents at opposite corners of the ring and start thinking of yourselves as a team. How can the two of you work together to achieve what you both want? After all, two heads are better than one, right?

8

My teenager thinks he is the boss

He has assumed the role and any attempt on my part to redress the balance ends up in bitter clashes.

In this chapter I will show you how you can redress the balance of power in your home. It is a really difficult situation when your child suddenly starts answering you back and telling you what to do. Most parents are so shocked when this happens that they are unsure where to start.

In most cases they do nothing or they try to gain back more control. Both of these are unlikely to have the desired effect. For parents who are going through this challenge, the daily struggles are frustrating and very demoralizing.

We will follow Tracy and Tim's journey as they try to redress the balance of power, and as they help their son Ryan to deal with his anger.

Case Study: Tracy, Tim and Ryan

....

Tracy and Tim came to me regarding their son Ryan. Ryan was just sixteen and a big lad at six feet two. He was very strong and over-powering and he ran the house. He dictated what they ate, when they went to bed, when they went out and what they did at the weekends. He ordered the rest of the house around, including his twelve-year-old sister, telling them everything from 'clean up your room,' to 'Mum, we are going out to eat tonight.' When they disagreed or challenged him he would just scream and shout and the house would erupt into a battleground. This usually resulted in his younger sister crying in her room, Tim having to leave the house for fear of what he would do to Ryan, mum with a splitting headache and Ryan slamming the door and storming out. Tracy and Tim could not understand it. They had always been very liberal and really, Ryan was living the perfect life for most teenagers. He was pretty much allowed to do what he wanted. They were very 'new age' with him. Their house was partly a haven, with people coming and going as they pleased. It was almost like a commune and was on the Devon coast, so why the difficulty?

The situation in this home is one I have seen many times before. When we bring up our children we generally do so in the way that we were brought up or in the way we would have wanted. We do not always take into account our children as individuals. We often bring up all our children the same way and then wonder why we have problems. Tracy and Tim were very liberal and free-minded and they were bringing Ryan up in the same way. However, Ryan himself was very disciplined and structured and was screaming out for some sort of boundaries and routine in his life. Because he could not find them he had taken it on his own shoulders to whip the family into shape. Each of your children needs bringing up in a different way and what works with one may not work with another. Take time to work out which way your child needs to be handled.

So the first thing I asked them was, 'Why do you think Ryan is like this?' They were at a loss, they really did not know. As far as they were concerned they were giving him a life that most of his friends envied. I then asked them to describe Ryan to me. Ryan was a protective young man with a sense of humour, at his best apparently really adorable. He was respectful, kind and loving apart from these outbursts. He was good at sport and was a keen boxer. He had been having some problems at school but they now seemed to be resolved. He wanted to go into the Marines after leaving school and was a really nice young fellow.

Part of your job as a parent is to teach your children about responsibility and independence. The best way to do this is by having very clear and concise boundaries and agreements in the home. A boundary is like a rule but much more fluid and flexible and it is reached by the parent and the child coming to agreements. A rule is issued and adhered to; a boundary is discussed and agreed. If you want a teenager to be supportive of what you are trying to do in the home, then you must include them in this process. To simply issue instructions is unlikely to get you anywhere.

The first piece of homework I gave the two of them was to have a conversation with Ryan and ask him how he preferred to be treated. A strange question, you may think, but I believe you should be asking your children this from a very early age. If you don't get what you ask for the first time, just ask it in a different way. For example, 'What do you need from me as a parent?' Tracy and Tim did as I suggested and after an initial, 'Well, you should know, you are my parents,' he came back with one request and that was, 'You should be teaching me what is right and wrong and what I can and can't do.' Ryan was clearly telling his parents that he wanted boundaries (and you would be surprised by how many teenagers say this). They may complain and moan when the boundaries are in place but secretly they do want to know what they can and cannot do.

When Tracy and Tim came back we looked at what Ryan had said. Remembering that they are very liberal we had to devise something that would work for them too. Since they were really allowing their children to do whatever they wanted, they did not know where to start. I suggested that they set their boundaries for the following:

1. Eating
2. Sleeping
3. Responsibilities – these were to include jobs and chores
4. Money
5. Behaviour.

Then I suggested that they find at least one boundary they could put in place under each heading.

A week later they came back with the following list:

1. As a family we all eat one meal a day together.
2. Each family member is responsible for going to bed at a time that allows them to get up refreshed in the morning.
3. Each person in the house is responsible for five household chores.
4. Each child is given £5 per month. The rest of their money comes from doing jobs or earning it for themselves.
5. We do not tolerate screaming and shouting in this house.

This list felt loose enough for them and structured enough for Ryan. I suggested that they show it to Ryan and ask if he had anything to add. Of course, Ryan did have things to add and most of what he added gave the contract more structure. They were happy with it, made agreements and it was adopted. They displayed the list in the house and looked at ways in which they would have to change their lifestyle to fit in with the new rules.

After coming to agreements on boundaries in the home you must follow them up. You have to make sure that your child knows what will happen if agreements are broken. I prefer to avoid the word 'punishment' in this context as I don't think we necessarily have a right to punish anyone; that is for the judges in this land, and anyway, I am not sure that it promotes learning. I like to think in terms of remedies or penalties – the effects and results that may follow the actions or inactions of the child. For example, if he doesn't come to eat with you, the natural consequence is that his food will be cold. The remedy is that he will have to reheat it. If he doesn't put his clothes in the wash basket, the natural consequence is that they will not be washed. The penalty is that he wears dirty clothes and the remedy will be that he has to wash them himself.

A penalty or remedy, following a natural consequence, should promote learning and teach the child about responsibility. It is important that we let our children know what natural consequences may follow a certain action or inaction and what penalties or remedies may be incurred because of that. Always make sure that your teenager knows, if a penalty or remedy is necessary, that its terms are understood: how long it will last, when it will start and how it will be carried out. You must stand really firm on this and be true to your word. If you never enforce a penalty or remedy, then the teenager will never learn about responsibility.

So Tracy and Tim went to Ryan with the expanded list of 'agreements' that they had made as a family, and explained to Ryan that they were going to sit down and discuss what would happen if any were broken. Ryan moaned and did not look too happy (as any teenager would), however, Tracy and Tim continued. They did as they said and agreed with him what would happen if agreements were broken. For example, if a person chose not to eat with the family then another meal would not be cooked for them. If Ryan did not get up in the mornings his mum would set his bedtime for a few weeks. If chores did not get done money was not paid. They wrote down all the consequences on another sheet and all signed it.

Inevitably Ryan did slip up. For three weeks he did really well and then on week four he just rebelled and refused to do anything. He would not eat with them, was going to bed at ridiculous hours, was not doing any chores and was screaming and shouting.

FREEZE: WHAT WOULD YOU HAVE DONE? ··········
Would you have shouted back? Grounded him? Given in? Or
just accepted it was par for the course?

Teenagers will rebel, they will test you and they will see how far
they can push the boundaries. The more you give in, the more they
will continue to test. They really are asking you to show them where
the limits are. They are learning how they can affect others and
are testing this out on you. Remember who the adult is and do not
give in – **the minute you give in they have won.** Your teenager
needs firmness from you. In order for his behaviour to continue, he
needs something to rebel against. If you maintain your firmness and
are strong, he will stop what he is doing as it gets him nowhere.

Tracy did not like conflict. She was distressed when she called me, she
did not know what to do and was all too happy just to give in. The most
important thing was that she did not give in. Ryan was testing her to see
how far he could push her; he was testing out the boundaries, rebelling
just for the sake of it, as teenagers do. Her job was to stay firm and calm
and to continue as agreed.

Tracy and I devised a system to deal with the fact that Ryan was
shouting at her. We called it '1, 2, 3, look at me' and it went like this:

1. Tell them what they are doing.
2. Tell them they are breaking an agreement you have made.
3. Tell them you are not going to change your mind.

Ask them to look at you, then tell them to stop it. Note here that it does not matter whether they look at you or not, so say it only once and continue.

So in practice it went:

1. 'Ryan, you are shouting at me.'
2. 'By shouting at me you are breaking one of the agreements we made.'
3. 'Shouting will not make me change my mind.'

So Tracy went off and tried the system with Ryan and he stopped shouting. Tracy had never been as strict as this with Ryan and it certainly was having an impact. For a few days all was well and he stuck to all the rules. Then on day three he refused to eat with the family, went out and then came home at 9pm nagging Tracy to cook him something to eat.

Tracy did not engage with him; she just went straight into the system she now had and it worked.

Ryan stormed off to his bedroom and Tracy called me, pleased as punch with herself. However, she also felt extremely guilty about the fact that he had had no dinner, a crisis faced by most parents.

Don't allow yourself to feel guilty. Make a distinction in your head between slave and parent. Parents so often say in jest to their children, 'And what did your last slave die of?' and never were more apt words spoken. You are not a slave, you are a parent with your own life and your own responsibilities. Your main job is to teach them to be responsible and by pandering to their every whim you will not build up responsibility. You can give in sometimes but be really careful. Backing down on rules and agreements you have set can undo all the good work you have done. Remember, when you feel guilty it is all about you and not your teenagers. They are old enough to take care of themselves and if they are hungry they can eat. They are not like smaller children who are dependent on you. They can actually look after themselves. Don't get wrapped up in their story about how hard done by they are and how you are a bad parent.

Getting back to Tracy, I had to get a piece of paper and write on it in big letters the word 'Guilty'. She then divided the paper in two. On one side she wrote all the positives about feeling guilty and then wrote all the negatives on the other side. On the positive side she wrote that it made her caring and always wanting to do her best. On the negative side it made her do things that were not in her best interests. After she had done this I simply asked, 'Do you still feel guilty about him not eating?' She replied with a resounding 'No'.

So Tracy and Tim continued with the system and all went well. Ryan even gave them a few penalties when they did not stick to the agreements. They had to be ready for this as it was, after all, only fair and part of the system. Things were much better and the house was a more peaceful place to be in. Ryan had stopped ordering everyone around. However, there were still a few occasions when his temper needed controlling. It looked as if it was time for some anger management.

To me, anger management is a tool to help people to manage their own emotions, whatever they may be. It follows three steps.

1. Know what the signs are.
2. Know what your breaking or boiling point is and what triggers you.
3. Find other ways to let the anger out.

To demonstrate this I use a 'temperature gauge' to help people in assessing their anger.

When you think of anger management for a teenager, I want you also to think of it for yourself. The teenager needs to be aware of what he is doing and you as a parent need to be aware of where your child's and your own trigger points are. When you know all this you can decrease the conflict in the house by walking away and leaving the situation when you or your teenager reaches boiling point.

The Anger Thermometer

What is it and how does it work?

It is in essence just like a thermometer, a line going from zero to ten.

o——————————————————————————————10

'o' is at the point where the teenager is not angry at all and '10' is full-blown riot stage.

When he knows where he is on the scale he can then begin to control the anger.

So let me show you how this worked with Ryan. I spent a day with him and his parents and they each did one. Below are the answers Ryan gave me and the results of drawing up his 'anger thermometer'.

I drew the line as above on a very large piece of paper and then asked Ryan, 'If zero is where you are not angry and ten is where you are out of control, at what point along the scale do you think you begin to lose control?'

Ryan said 'six'.

'What happens when you are at six?'

'I shout and scream and punch things and I want to just get out of the house.'

'Tell me what happens in your body before you get to six.'

'I begin to clench my fists and I can feel myself getting hot.'

'At what number does this happen?'

'Five.'

'What happens just before you get to five?'

'I start telling my mum it is unfair and I nag her – I am at a four then.'

'What has been said to you just before that point?'

'My mum says "no" or disagrees with me. I keep asking and she just keeps saying "no". This is at about three.'

'So at what point do you think you could do something different?'

'About three or four.'

'How could you let the anger out at three or four without harming yourself or someone else?'

'I could go up to my room and punch my punchbag and think of a better way to get my point across.'

'What questions could you ask yourself?'

'Why am I angry? What do I really want? How can I get it in a more positive way?'

As you can see from this, Ryan was in control of himself at three and four. Once he reached five he was beginning to lose control and at six he had no hope of returning. It also gave us clues about when mum should back off. If Ryan was nagging her then it was an indication to her that he was going up the scale and she had a choice, either to carry on or to put a stop to what was happening. What we also learn is that it took Ryan a full two hours to get from three to six so mum and dad had plenty of time to work with him and calm him down.

I did the same exercise with Tracy and Tim and shared the results with Ryan so as a family they could all work together. They worked hard for a week, recognizing the triggers and then backing down and supporting each other to manage their own emotions. They even had a funny saying that let them all know that the person was going up the temperature gauge and it was, 'Hey, cool it honey,' in a very American voice. Most of the time it did the trick as they all fell about laughing.

Over the next few months, things in the house improved greatly. They continued to have the occasional screaming match, Ryan still broke the agreements sometimes, but all in all things improved. It was time for me to leave them to it. When we had started the coaching Ryan had been in charge of the house. Now, after four months, we had redressed the balance and instead of any one person being in charge they worked together as a team. I asked Tracy and Tim what they had learnt most and they said without hesitation, 'Everyone is different and we need to treat them as such.'

Action Points

....

1. Decide that enough is enough!

Decide now that you are no longer willing to accept this kind of behaviour. Any time your teenager bosses you around from now on, refuse to play ball and don't listen. Don't respond to commands and threats and don't be a push-over. Your teenage alien needs to learn the score and it won't happen if you are pandering to him. Make a stand and stick to it.

2. Ask for feedback.

If your teenager has taken over, then it may be because he is not getting what he wants or needs from you. Be very brave and ask your teenager how he wants to be treated. Ask him what he wants and whether you are doing well or badly. Imagine if your boss at work asked you how you liked to be managed. Would that feel good?

Remember, if we want to get the best out of someone then we need to be willing to find out how to do it. The question you need to be thinking is, 'How can I be the best parent for my son or daughter?' You know you don't have all the answers – perfection is not the aim here. Be courageous and ask them. If the worst comes to the worst and they don't answer, well, at least you may have stunned them into silence for a while.

3. Set boundaries.

However much teenagers wriggle, complain and break boundaries, they do actually want them. They may never admit to that but it is true. Set some boundaries in your house; not too many, I think five is a really good number. Try these categories.

1. Eating
2. Sleeping
3. Responsibilities (include jobs and chores)
4. Money
5. Behaviour.

To give these even more impact, sit down with your teenager and discuss them. Tell him that you want to put some new boundaries in place that encourage responsibility and you want him to help you with them. That way he will feel more committed to the process. If he refuses, just tell him that you will do them anyway and he can always discuss them with you later. Make sure that the boundaries are clear and precise. Be willing to negotiate a little until all the family are happy and make it clear that if someone needs to break a boundary, for whatever reason, they should seek agreement first. For example, your teenager may need to go to music practice as a one-off on the night that you have as family night. Let that be agreed.

Make a list now of your five Top Boundaries, write them on a large piece of paper and put it in a prominent place – I always like the kitchen or hall. If your family will sign the list, encourage them to do so. Also be clear that these boundaries apply to you too!

4. Discuss consequences.

Discuss as a family what the penalties or remedies will be for breaking the boundaries or agreements that you have made together, just as Tracy and Tim did. Don't make them open ended. Make sure everyone knows for how long the penalties will last. 'If you don't get up for school then I will set your bedtime for the next two weeks.' Make a list now of penalties that you think may be suitable if your boundaries are broken and make a date to discuss them with the rest of the family.

5. Claim back some power.

Stick to your guns and be consistent. If agreements are broken, speak up and don't let them go unnoticed. Use the '1, 2, 3, look at me' system.

1. Tell them what they are doing.
2. Tell them which rule or agreement they are breaking.
3. Tell them you are not going to change your mind.

Tell your teenager to look you in the eyes and then tell him to stop it.

So if your teenager breaks a curfew, the next day you would say to him:

1. 'Last night you came in after your curfew.'
2. 'You have broken one of the agreements that we put in place and therefore a penalty will be issued.'

3. 'For the next week you will be in at 8pm and I will not ch
   my mind.'
4. 'Look at me . . . it is not acceptable for you to break you
   do not do it again.'

Remember, whether he looks at you or not is immaterial – it is just saying the words that counts.

6. Deal with the 'guilt attack'.

Yes, at some time your teenager is going to send you on a massive guilt trip. When you take some of his power back he will try everything and guilt is normally his first line of defence. Don't give in, stay firm after all the hard work you have done. Get a piece of paper now and divide it into two columns. Write the word 'Guilt' across the top. On the left side write all the good things about your guilt, all the positive things it brings to you. On the right side write the negative things – what does feeling guilty make you do that you do not want to do? Keep this piece of paper safe and when you get a 'guilt attack' get it out, read it and add to it. Your subconscious will soon get the message. You are not a slave.

7. Keep your emotions in check.

Many households are ruled by emotions, be they anger, fear or sadness. We are each driven by one more than the other. How about your teenager? Use the anger thermometer with yourself, get used to your own trigger points and put things in place that enable you to manage your emotions first. You need to be able to do it for yourself first before you have any hope of doing it with your teenager. Then look closely at him. Where are his trigger points, when can you back off? Observe him and help him work out how he can control himself. If he will not let you do the anger thermometer with him, you can almost do it for him. Knowing him as you do, you will be able to see the signs. Copy this part of the book and leave it for him – he may read it. Start now to understand your own and your teenager's emotions and put in place ways to manage them.

8. The family business

Stop thinking who is boss and start thinking as a team. Think of it as a company. You are the Chief Executive and you need your team to be on your side, working with you so that the company can achieve success. Stop thinking about how you can control your teenager to get what you want. Start thinking about how you can all work together to achieve success as a family.

9

My teenager will not listen to my advice

How can I get her to listen to me as intently and with the same conviction as she listens to her friends?

During this chapter I will show you how you can become influential in your child's life and help them in making positive choices. It is not a chapter where I show you how to get your teenager to listen and do what you want.

As parents we want our teenagers to do the 'right' things and make the 'right' choices. We don't want them to make the same mistakes that we made. We want to give them the experience of our wisdom but we cannot get them to listen. So as you read through this chapter stop thinking, 'How can I get my teenager to do what I want?' and start thinking, 'How can I help my teenager to make a choice that is positive and supportive of whom they want to become?'

We will follow Marie's journey as she helps her daughter Sharmain to make important decisions about her future.

Case Study: Marie and Sharmain

....

Marie came to me about her daughter Sharmain. Sharmain was sixteen and had her own opinions about how she wanted to live her life. She did not want to go to college, could not see the point and would refuse to discuss it.

FREEZE: WHAT WOULD YOU HAVE DONE? ········
Would you give her the 'if you want to get a good job you must go to college' lecture, give up on her as a no-hoper, ground her until she comes to her senses, or ignore it as a 'passing trend'?

....

Marie was devastated because she had hoped that Sharmain would make more of her life than she herself had. She had tried in vain many times to get Sharmain to listen to her and it did not seem to matter what she did, Sharmain took no notice of her but listened to her friends intently, always took on board what they said and changed her mind easily. In fact, it was after her best friend had decided not to go to college that Sharmain decided not to go either. Marie just wanted to be influential in her daughter's life. She wanted her to listen and take note. Because of her own experiences, she did not want Sharmain to make the same mistakes.

Marie was like many parents I come across. She felt very distant from her daughter, did not know how to influence her decisions and felt helpless. It is devastating for us as parents when we realize that we do not have any influence over our precious children, that actually they are young adults, that they are grown up and we have no control over them whatsoever. This can be a very frightening experience. As parents we need to remember that **we are raising independent human beings who can think and make decisions for themselves. We are not making clones of ourselves to live our unfulfilled dreams through.**

It was obvious to me that this is what Marie was trying to do. I simply said to her, 'Who are you doing it for?' 'Well, Sharmain of course,' she said. 'And how will you feel if Sharmain does not fulfill her potential?' 'Awful,' she said. 'I will feel as if I have failed, as if I am a bad parent, as if she is going to have the same life as I had, as if I am no good.' 'So who are you doing it for?' I asked again. She paused and said, 'I don't understand what you mean.' 'I just wondered if you were doing it for Sharmain's sake or your own sake.' She stopped as she realized what she was doing. 'Oh,' she said, 'you're right, I am doing this for me not for her. In fact, who am I to know what is right for her?' So I sent Marie away with some homework about the college decision. I asked her to write a list of all the reasons why Sharmain not going to college worried her, and what the worst situation would be if she did not.

Don't assume that your teenager will make the same mistakes as you. Remember that you are different people with different backgrounds, different skills and different ways of thinking. You differ in as many ways as you resemble each other. Don't assume that because your teenager makes a decision that you don't agree with, the outcome will be the worst thing that could happen. Remember that she is a different person, she is not who you were at that age.

Marie came back with her list, which included:

1. Sharmain was going to doss around doing nothing.
2. She would get pregnant.
3. She would have a bad life just like her mother did.
4. Without a degree and a good job she was not going to be able to look after Marie in her later life.

Marie was shocked by some of the things she had written. It was obvious to her that she did not trust her daughter and she was assuming that she was going to make the same mistakes that she herself had made and that, yet again, she would be picking up the pieces as she has in her own life. Marie was telling herself a whole story about what not going to college meant for Sharmain and it was governing her life.

We then looked together at what made her and her daughter alike and what made them different. Their similarities included their compassion, their rebellious nature and their ability to have a good time. Their differences included the fact that Sharmain was very outspoken and strong, had lots of friends and lots of support and was very confident. As we did this, Marie began to realize that they were entirely different people and just because Sharmain made a similar choice to Marie it did not necessarily mean that the outcome would be the same.

The next thing Marie and I did together was to hold a brainstorming session, thinking of all the reasons why Sharmain should not go to college, as well as all the many different ways her future could work out. This helped Marie to open her mind to all the other possible outcomes and it gave her hope that everything could work out well.

Marie was feeling some relief over the college decision and no longer felt that Sharmain had to take her advice. She had for the last few weeks stopped 'nagging' Sharmain and as a result their relationship had improved. Sharmain was even asking her opinion on a few things – which was unheard of before. It felt as if it was time to move on. I said to Marie, 'What is it you want for Sharmain?' 'Well, I just want her to know that I am here to support her should she need it.' We had a good starting point. So the first thing I asked Marie to do was to be bold, and to go home and ask her daughter if she felt that her mother supported her.

 TIME OUT ....

When you think of support in relation to your teenager I want you to think in terms of five specific areas.

1. Financial
2. Emotional
3. Physical
4. Intellectual
5. Spiritual.

We often only think of Financial and Emotional, forgetting the others which are just as important.

....

Marie asked Sharmain if she felt supported and got the answer that she expected, which was, 'No, you just nag and nag me and you want me to do what you want, not what I want.' This was no surprise to either of us because that is precisely what Marie had been doing. So I told Marie to go back and say to Sharmain, 'I really want to help you when you make your decisions without interfering – would you be willing to talk to me about it?' Marie did this and to her surprise Sharmain said, 'Yes, as long as you don't do your "when I was a kid" line and go into all the doom and gloom about what might happen.'

Marie and Sharmain had a long conversation, during most of which Marie had her lips firmly closed. She found out so much about her daughter, including how creative she was and how the structured school environment did little for her. She learned about her interest in food and her skills at talking to people. What she learnt surprised her and she realized that the decision Sharmain was making was probably the best one for her. Marie wanted to know how she could offer her support so that Sharmain would see that she would be there for her.

We decided that Marie would take Sharmain away for a weekend. During that time they would devise a plan together using the five areas I had given in relation to support. Marie said to Sharmain, 'I enjoyed speaking with you the other day about your plans for the future. I would love to spend more time with you chatting about this. I was thinking that we could go away for a spa weekend – what do you think?' Well, of course Sharmain jumped at the chance. Marie and I then went through the five areas and I instructed her to ask just five questions of Sharmain the whole time. They were:

1. How can I help you to work out the financial implications of what you want to do? (Financial)
2. How can I help you with your worries? (Emotional)

3. How can I help you find out what you need to know? (Intellectual)

4. How can I help you in making your decisions fit in with your plans for your life? (Spiritual)

5. How can I help you get yourself physically ready for what you are hoping to achieve? (Physical)

The few days they spent away were encouraging. Marie just let Sharmain talk about her plans and her dreams. It seemed that she wanted to open her own organic restaurant. Her plans were promising and she was excited. Marie asked all the questions she needed to and was careful not to judge or ask any more. The questions may not have come out totally as above but she got her point across. They had never talked so much before and Marie was very happy. It appeared the support Sharmain needed was for Marie to countersign a loan, so that she could go to stay with a friend in California (which was full of the type of restaurant she wanted to open), and see how they did it over there. She was trying to get herself a work placement in one of the restaurants so she could learn as much as she could before coming back to this country.

 FREEZE: WHAT WOULD YOU HAVE DONE? ········
Are you panicking and thinking you would never do that? Is your heart beating faster and a slight sweat beginning to form on your forehead? Or are you understanding and supportive like Marie?

Marie agreed to the loan and laid out strict guidelines for repayment. It appeared that Sharmain had already worked out a plan.

The next few months that Sharmain had at school were the most productive she had ever had and her previously failed 'mocks' gave way to 'C' and 'B' grades. The whole summer was spent with her mum organizing her trip, which was to start in September. Every time she had a worry she would come to her mum. She spent less time in her bedroom talking to her friends about things that she could not previously speak to her mum about.

Marie had learnt so much by setting her daughter free. She had learnt how creative she really was and how talented and driven she was. By stopping interfering she has allowed her daughter to show her mum how great she is. There was little left for me to do. Marie could do it by herself now.

The transformation in Marie's household had really been very short in comparison to some of the other situations in this book. The turnaround had taken about three months and most of this was due to the fact that Marie had 'let go' and given her daughter room to shine, to show her mum that she was responsible and could make good decisions. Marie had become influential in her daughter's life again and Sharmain discussed her plans and hopes with her. Interestingly enough, what happened in this situation was that Sharmain decided to go to catering college before going to California and is at present doing a catering management degree. Her grades had improved so much that she decided that college would be a good option, giving her a good way of moving forward with her plans. She still intends to make the trip to California when she finishes college. Funny isn't it? By letting go parents can sometimes get the outcome they want anyway!

Action Points

....

1. Stop thinking advice and start thinking relationship.

Stop thinking, 'How can I get her to listen to my advice?' and start thinking, 'How can I build a relationship with her so that I can become influential and she will want to talk to me and ask for my support?'

2. She is not you!

Make sure that you are not trying to live the life you did not have through your teenager. Your teenager is not you, she is her own person and that is how you need to treat her. You are not raising a teenager to lead the life or do the job/profession that you think is acceptable. You are raising a unique individual. Let her be that. Make a list now of all the things you want for your teenager, the job you would want her to have, the life you would want her to lead and then throw it away! Ask yourself a better question. 'How do I want my child to feel while she is living her life?' You will realize that really, you just want her to be happy and only she will know how to find happiness.

3. What is the worst thing that could happen?

Get a pen and paper and write down the worst thing that could happen in this situation, the thing you are worried about the most –

the story you are telling yourself. Put a plan in place that you can put into action should the very worst happen. This will help to reassure you and will also make you realize that even if it does happen you will be ready!

4. Manage yourself first.

Bringing up a child, remember, is all about managing yourself first. **Note to yourself – all the worrying is all about you really, not your child.** Look at your own feelings and worries about your child and ask what you can do to ease them. What support is needed, what systems do you need to put in place?

5. You are the same but different.

Just because your teenager may be making what you think is the wrong decision, this does not mean that it will end up as badly as you may think. Make a list of all the ways that you and your teenager are the same and all the ways that you are different. How might your teenager deal with a situation in a different way? What skills does she have that will help her in this situation? Has she dealt with similar situations before that have had a positive ending? What comfort can you gain by examining how she has dealt with situations in the past?

6. Open up to possibilities.

Brainstorm all the possible outcomes of the decisions she is making. We mostly panic when we think that there is only one choice or one way something will end up. Open your mind to the other possibilities. Get a piece of paper and a pen now and think of at least twenty possible outcomes to the situation, then think of another ten. For extra reference, ask your teenager how she thinks this situation will turn out.

7. Support, support, support

Now you can see this situation more clearly. Get out of 'rescue mode', (yes, things may go wrong and that is okay) and into 'support mode'. Start asking your teenager what support she needs rather than trying to influence her decisions. Look at the five areas of support and ask yourself how you fare. Be brave and ask your teenager how she thinks you fare. When your teenager is making decisions think of support questions that you can ask in the five areas:

1. Financial
2. Emotional
3. Physical
4. Intellectual
5. Spiritual.

8. Allow your teenager to talk.

Spend time just listening. I mean really listening to your teenager – to her hopes and her fears. Keep your lips closed and just listen. Make every day a learning opportunity where you will find out how good your teenager is just by listening to her. Start with five minutes a day and keep increasing it, heading for thirty to sixty. If she will not speak with you for that long, don't worry, just listen intently in the time you have.

9. Let the goodness shine through.

Look at your teenager with different eyes, see how good she is, believe that she can and will make the right decisions. Step back and stop trying to influence. Give her an 'A+' in decision-making and know that she will succeed if only you allow it. This is, after all, why teenagers listen to their friends so much, because they believe in them.

10

My teenager lives in a single-parent household and I'm sure that it is affecting her

How do I become both mother and father to her during these turbulent years? How can I show her I am strong and independent while also still being a good mother?

The purpose of this chapter is to show single parents how they can ease the stress and feel less exhausted at the end of each day. Being a single parent of a teenager can be challenging, the violent mood swings and outbursts can become difficult to handle, especially if you are all alone. However, this does not only apply to single parents. Parents with partners can also feel alone sometimes, isolated and weak when dealing with their teenager, and this chapter will help them too.

When we are single parents it is important that we maintain healthy relationships with our children while still providing the structure and support that would be provided by two parents.

We will follow Natalie's journey as she tries to bring some structure into her home and to address the balance of power.

Case Study: Natalie and Sam

Meet Natalie, mother to Sam. They have been alone since Sam's father left when she was three. At fifteen, Sam appeared to have adopted the 'other adult role' in the house, questioning Natalie at every juncture about what she was doing and where she was going. Natalie was not allowed a minute's peace and had no privacy. When Natalie came to me she was blaming herself for Sam's obsessive behaviour. She believed that Sam was taking advantage of her purely because there was not a man in the house. It was clear to me that the roles and balance of power in this house were not as they ought to be.

Parents who have a very close relationship with their children can lean on them too much for emotional support and get too clingy and dependent on them. (This aspect of the single parent/child relationship can be equally important but it is not dealt with specifically in this chapter because the emphasis has to be on what I found with Natalie and Sam.) Children can also become too clingy and dependent on the parents. In both situations the result is that the child does not learn to grow into an adult and be their own person. This can happen more in single-parent homes since there is not another adult in the house. The parent tells all her worries and concerns to her child and the child soon learns to listen and protect. What needs to happen in these situations is a clear division and distinction between the roles in the house.

I felt that I needed to get a bird's-eye view of Natalie and Sam's situation so I moved in for a week.

What I found really shocked me. It was like watching an old married couple. Sam and Natalie did not communicate like mother and daughter, they were so close that they were almost inseparable. Natalie relied on Sam too much and quite often would play a 'child role'. Consequently, Sam had learnt that she needed to 'protect' her mum and really would not let her do anything. Natalie saw Sam as the strong one and Sam saw Natalie as weak. All Natalie did was to play at being 'mum'. All Sam ever saw was her mum doing things directly for her. It was no surprise that she treated Natalie like a doormat.

TIME OUT

Being a mother is a full-time job and for a single mother there is no let up. You are entirely responsible and have to be vigilant all the time as you and you alone take full responsibility for your child. It is important to remember that there is more to life than just being a parent. It is, after all, just one of the roles that you play in your life. There are other roles: you may also be a daughter, an employee, a lover or a friend. When we realize that we are more than just a parent it enables us to do and be more. **You are the best role model your child has** and if you want her to be happy and successful (which I know you do) then you need to ensure that you are being the role model for that success.

I needed to help Natalie to see that she was an individual, leading her own life. To make her stronger as a parent we needed her to be stronger as a person. The first thing I asked Natalie to do was to define the roles that she had. She said she was parent, employee, friend, daughter and individual. We then went on to describe all these roles, what they involved and how she wanted to behave within each one. For example, as a parent she described her role as helping her daughter to become independent, and being firm but fair, loving and consistent. As an individual she described this as nurturing herself, her creativity, and having fun. For this she needed to be brave and courageous. Natalie now realized that there was more to her life than just being a single parent. She had identified with it and all its negative aspects for so long that she was unable to appreciate anything else. She needed to give herself permission to be herself and to follow her own dreams too. When we spoke about this Natalie appeared anxious. When I asked her what was wrong she said, 'I don't want Sam to feel I have abandoned her.'

Some single parents can over-compensate out of guilt. This can be exhausting and lead to over-parenting or over-protection. In fact, some single parents are much more attentive than couples since they have no one else to occupy their time. It can leave children feeling trapped and unsure about who they are or what role they play in the family. It is important that single parents find someone who they can talk to, who they trust and can turn to when they feel the need to scream. They need someone to call upon so that they do not feel tempted to off-load their troubles onto their child.

Getting Natalie stronger was not going to be easy. She felt guilty most of the time, and this guilt was driving most of the decisions she made. With no one to discuss this with she inevitably gave in to the guilt. She quite often unloaded on Sam her feelings of being a bad parent, with very little support around her and no one to really talk to about it. I stepped in as 'confidante'. We decided that for a few months she was to call me every time she felt guilty, exhausted or just not sure what to do.

Natalie would call me most nights in tears about something that had happened. She kept saying, 'If there was a man in the house she would not behave like this.' One evening I asked her what she thought a man would bring to the house that was not there already. She went into a long list which included words such as control, discipline, structure and order. Natalie equated men with all the power words.

Natalie was making excuses for the problems in her house. She believed that a fairy tale or a happy ending might exist and that a man would come and sweep her off her feet and carry her away, making everything all right. Sam would be happy and start behaving and all would be well. Most parents want a magic wand or a miracle to happen but it just does not work like that. Making excuses and wishing mean that you give yourself permission to not be responsible and take action. To turn a teenager around you actually need to do something, however hard that may seem. You have to decide whether the excuses will win or whether you will win. Natalie needed to stop thinking that a man would solve her problems and to start taking action.

I asked Natalie, 'What makes you think that as a woman you cannot do these things?' 'Well, it is not what we are good at, is it?' she replied. 'Have you ever tried it?' I asked. 'Well, no,' Natalie said gingerly. When I asked her how she knew she could not do it, there was silence. The fact was she didn't know. I then asked her to write a list, during the next couple of days, of all the ways in which she thought a man could help – the times when she told herself, 'Sam would not do this if there was a man in the house.' When Natalie came back to me her list had four specific things on it. They were:

1. Shouting and swearing at me
2. Refusing to eat what I cook and treating me like a slave
3. Not leaving me alone when I want to speak with my friends
4. Constantly harassing me about where I am going.

 TIME OUT ....

In my experience of working with single parents I see similarities in their problems and they fall into these general categories:

1. A general lack of respect over small things, such as shouting and swearing, which if left can escalate into much bigger problems.
2. The parent over-compensating and doing too much for the child, and consequently the child expecting more and more to be done for them.
3. The child or parent being too 'involved' in the other's life.

These need to be nipped in the bud as early as possible or the parent will run into real problems in the future.

....

Natalie's list contained four problems that could be solved, without a man. We had to make plans to help her to regain some of the power that she felt was missing in the house. It was simple. All we needed to do was to try methods that would deal with each of her problems. One of the best ways to solve problems like these at home, is to devise methods which you can use frequently and consistently.

We decided to treat this as an experiment, with Natalie trying out a new method every week, evaluating them as we went along. If we did not see any improvement in three months I would believe what she said.

1. Shouting and swearing at me.

When Sam shouted we were going to implement the four-step approach.

1. Natalie was to tell her what she was doing.
2. She would ask her to stop it.
3. She would tell her how it made her feel.
4. She would tell her what she would do if it continued.

If Sam started shouting, Natalie was to say:

1. 'Sam, do you realize you are shouting at me?'
2. 'Please stop.'
3. 'When you shout at me it makes me feel angry.'
4. 'I feel that I don't want to help you if you continue to shout at me and I shall have to leave the room.'

When attempting to regain control in your home it is important to be clear and concise about what you want to achieve and to have a method that you can implement over and over again. When you speak to your teenager, make sure you speak slowly, clearly and in a neutral tone. She needs to know that you mean business. No shouting, whining voices or the meek and mild thing, it just will not do. Natalie had a way of speaking to Sam in these situations – what I called her 'little girl' voice – so we had to do a lot of training to get her to speak in a different way. Natalie invented an alter ego called 'Michelle'. Michelle was successful, confident; she was very business-like and just said things as they were. When Natalie needed to implement her strategies she thought of Michelle and adopted her role.

Natalie put this in place and for the most part all was well. At first, Sam said she didn't care that she was shouting. Then she started shouting back at her mother, then ignoring her. Eventually she gave in and stopped shouting.

2. Refusing to eat what I cook and treating me like a slave.

We made sure Sam did not treat Natalie as a slave. For example, a meal was cooked and put on the table: Sam was told it was ready and if she did not come down to eat it she would have to heat it up herself. Natalie did not heat the food up and did not cook anything else. Sam shouted, whined, told Natalie she was a bad mother and even threw the food at her one night. But Natalie stood firm, called me when she needed support and stayed consistent. After a few weeks of this Sam got the idea and just came to the table.

Consistency over a period of time is the key here. Did you know that most people will only try something new twice before they give up and believe it is not working? You may have to try dozens and dozens of times before you see any results. The important thing is not to give up. If you give up you may as well give in. Importantly, Natalie did not give in, she wanted things to change and she was prepared to put the time and effort in to make them happen.

Natalie felt more in control and less like needing a man around. She was finding it easier to deal with Sam; consequently Sam was behaving better and was easier to get along with.

3. Not leaving me alone when I want to speak with my friends

We agreed that if Sam interrupted her when she was on the phone, Natalie would put it down (as she did not want other people to hear her and Sam). She would then walk away from Sam and not engage with her at all. If Sam tried to engage with her she would say, 'Sam, I am angry with you because you would not let me talk in peace on the phone. When you are ready to allow me to make my call in peace then I will speak with you.' Sam hated this and at first would follow Natalie everywhere, asking her to speak with her. Apart from a few occasions, Natalie held firm and when Sam gave in, Natalie would make the call first before spending time with her. Sam soon got the message and stopped interrupting her.

However, Sam still appeared to think that they were inseparable. Because they had been alone for so long, Sam assumed the role that the father would and they quite often spent their evenings together just talking. This is all nice and fine but not when your child just wants you all to herself all the time. It was a habit that the two of them had got into and it needed to be broken slowly and gently. After all, Sam had been used to the way it had been for twelve years now. I asked Natalie what small things she could do to take a step forward. She came up with the following list:

1. Go out with a friend after work once a week.
2. Go for coffee at the gym before I come home.
3. Have an hour to myself at home.
4. Read in the evenings.
5. Have friends over.

We began to implement these little by little and Sam found it very difficult. There were many tantrums and screaming of, 'You don't love me!' but we remembered the reason why we were doing it and kept going.

4. Constantly harassing me about where I am going

However, things got really bad when Natalie told Sam that she was going out on a date. Sam had locked Natalie in the bathroom telling her that she could not come out until she said she was not going.

 FREEZE: WHAT WOULD YOU HAVE DONE? ⋯⋯⋯
Would you have cried, called the police, given in and said you were not going, or tried to find a different solution?

Natalie called me from the bathroom (not sure how she got her phone in there). She was crying, she wanted to give in and make the whole situation go away but she knew that was not the answer. We talked about how Sam may be feeling and what she may be thinking about the situation. Natalie realized that Sam may be feeling very scared that she was going to lose her mum. Natalie could also see that the way to deal with this situation was not by giving in but by attempting to understand. I asked Natalie to tell Sam that she was not going to change her mind, but that she really wanted to understand how Sam felt and could she come out so they could talk. After about ten more minutes Sam calmed down and let her out. While Sam was shouting Natalie refused to talk to her, just saying, 'Sam, when you shout at me I cannot hear what you are saying properly because I am angry that you are speaking to me like that. When you calm down we can talk.'

 TIME OUT
Sometimes the most powerful thing that you can do to improve any behaviour in your home is to try and understand how your teenager may be feeling. We must remember that teenagers are not as good at handling their emotions as we are and they cannot be rational about their feelings all the time. Screaming and shouting can be purely out of a feeling that they are not being listened to and understood. When we take the time to truly understand what is happening within them it is easier for us to arrive at solutions with them.

Eventually Sam calmed down and spilled the beans, saying how she thought her mum was not safe and that she worried she was going to love someone else more than her and that she would leave. Rather than trying to convince her that was not the case, Natalie asked Sam what she needed from her mother to make her feel better about the situation. After some discussion, they agreed that Sam could call her twice during the evening to make sure everything was fine, and that they would start to do something together once a week. If Natalie went on a second date with the man then Sam would be able to meet him.

You may not have done this and you may wonder why Natalie should. Really, she did not have to, but if she wanted to maintain the relationship with her daughter then she needed to listen and understand. *The relationship with Sam was more important to Natalie than winning.* The evening went well and when Natalie went on a second date with the man, Sam met him. Natalie continued to spend more and more time away from Sam and consequently, Sam spent more time with her own friends. After three months Natalie had to admit that I was right and that she didn't need a man in the house – she was strong and she could do what was necessary.

Natalie has transformed herself from someone who thought she was a victim into a strong, independent woman who has her own life and is not afraid to stand up for herself. This alone is what has helped the most in improving the situation at home. Their relationship is much better, they spent great times apart as well as together and for the most part Sam is respectful and understanding of her mother.

Action Points

1. Define your role.

Be clear that you are more than a single parent; don't let that be the way that you see yourself. Write down on a piece of paper all the roles you play. Then write down what each one means to you, what it involves and how you want to behave within it. Take a look at the parent role and name three things that you can change today that will make the biggest difference.

2. Become a good role model.

How can you be the best role model for your child? How can you show your child that you are an individual in your own right? How can you encourage her to be more of an individual?

3. Find an 'unloading buddy'.

Find someone who you can trust to unload on, daily if you have to. Someone who you will not feel guilty about calling and speaking with. Make a list of what you need from this person – what questions do you need them to ask you? Do they just need to remind you what it is you want? How can they support you to move toward your goal?

4. Compensate for the other parent.

If you feel that your child is not getting all they would from two parents, then take action. Make a list of all the things that you think the other parent would be providing. Then ask yourself how you can provide them and start doing it.

5. Take time for yourself.

You are important and you need time for yourself; time to do the things that you want to do and time to show your children that you can actually function without them. Carve out some time for yourself, small things that you can do daily and weekly.

11

My teenager appears to have such low self-esteem

She has no self-belief and just sits in her bedroom for hours, she is always falling out with her friends and is over-sensitive to what others say about her.

Low self-esteem, or low self-belief, can be really difficult for parents to deal with and in this chapter I will be giving you practical suggestions to use at home.

I believe that the way we think about and see ourselves has an effect on how we behave. What we have to do with low self-esteem is to ultimately change how the teenager feels about herself.

We will follow Louise as she tries to coax her fourteen-year-old daughter Katie out of her bedroom.

Case Study: Louise and Katie

When Louise came to me she was concerned about her daughter Katie. Katie spent most of her time in her bedroom, appeared to have very few friends, hardly ever went out, was scared of getting on public transport and was constantly obsessed with the way she looked. She was so sensitive and the slightest thing appeared to send her into a depression. Louise had taken her to the doctor, who said that there was nothing wrong with her and refused to give her medicine for depression. Louise did not know what to do. She felt that her daughter needed help and was at a loss as to how to help her. I asked Louise to bring Katie in to see me, which she did. Although Katie was definitely not one of the most confident girls I have ever seen it was also obvious to me that she was quite a shy and quiet type. The first thing I had to get Louise to realize here was that some of what she was trying to change was indeed part of Katie's personality. I asked Louise to write down all the things that she thought needed to change about Katie. Louise came back to me with the following list:

1. She has few friends.
2. She is always saying she is fat and no one likes her.
3. She doesn't go out.
4. She will not get on public transport.
5. She will not do anything that slightly scares her.
6. She is so sensitive.

We looked at the list together and I asked, 'Louise, which of these could be part of her personality, part of who she is?' After a long pause Louise said, 'Perhaps she is just not a very sociable person.' 'Is this difficult for you to accept?' I asked. 'Well yes, I guess I am so outgoing and have so much fun and I just want Katie to be the same.' So here we had Louise's first insight. There were some things about her daughter that she found uncomfortable, things that she may just have to get used to, things that were part of who Katie was.

As parents we need to be aware that some personalities are more reserved and like to be alone. Often, parents are simply worried because their teenage girls are not acting as they would have done, or in the way they think they should act. So first you need to be very clear – is your teenager daughter suffering from low self-esteem or is she just not doing what you would have done?

Louise had realized that she needed to accept some of Katie's better qualities. I asked her to make a list of all her daughter's personality traits that she found difficult to understand, and to look at why they may be good. Louise admitted that actually, because Katie was not very sociable, she was likely to do better in her exams and not get into so much trouble. Also, she was more likely to have a few very close friends. We then looked at the things that we could work on with Katie:

1. Relationships with friends
2. The way she saw herself
3. Her fear of public transport and anything else that frightened her
4. The way she dealt with her sensitivity.

When helping your teenager to start to feel better about herself you need to ensure that whatever you do is fairly low key. In my experience, you need to take one small step at a time and not to expect massive leaps forward very quickly. Part of what you are dealing with is a teenager just making sense of herself, who she is and what she wants to be as an adult. Being a 'nearly adult' can be daunting, and when she realizes that soon she will have to go it alone she may switch off and revert to more childish behaviour than before. You need to offer support and not be panicked by what she says or does unless it becomes dangerous. Essentially, you are helping your teenager to get a real sense of herself, who she is and what she stands for.

1. Relationships with friends

This can sometimes be the most difficult. Katie's problem appeared to be that her friends changed like the wind and one day she had four, the next day she had one. It didn't appear to be her lack of making them, it was keeping them. I suggested to Louise that instead of telling her off, she should start asking questions every time Katie came home with a sob story about a friend. In this way she would find out more about the situation and what she could learn from it. If Katie had fallen out with Jade this week, what had Jade done? What had Katie done? As Louise continued to do this she learnt more about Katie and how she wanted her friends to be – honest, non-judgemental of others, caring, fun to be with and attentive to her. If a friend spoke about another person in front of her she was upset, if one of her friends inadvertently left her out she was upset, if one of her friends did not ask her what was wrong she was upset. Katie was making the mistake that most adults make, let alone teenagers. She was not asking herself what she wanted in a friend and she was not confronting her friends when they did something she found difficult. Katie clearly found confrontation very difficult and would rather stay quiet than cause a scene or speak out. Since we had learnt so much information we could now help her with some suggestions.

I went to see Katie and we implemented a 'Full-fat, Half-fat' system for her friends. A strange name, I know, but Katie thought of it. Together, we made up a list of ten qualities that she wanted in a friend, including the ones her mum had uncovered above. We scored each friend out of ten, depending on how they displayed these qualities. A full-fat friend was anyone who scored over eight and these were people that she really wanted to be with. Half-fat friends scored five and below, and these were ones that she did not want to spend as much time with. Friends between five and eight she called semi-skimmed, and these were ones who you liked but would not want as best friends. Katie discovered that she only had two friends that scored eight or more out of ten. I did not tell Katie to do anything, I just left her with the information and said I would allow her to make up her mind what to do with it.

If you have a relationship with your teenager where you can do this then you have an advantage. If not, the easiest way to get this point across is to talk about your own friends, what you like about them, what you don't like about them, why you spend more time with one than the other. This will help her to learn how to understand the information. When she falls out with a friend you can say things like, 'Well, Natalie can be very judgemental; perhaps that is why you find her difficult to be with.' Help her to make sense of all the emotions she feels about her friends and let her know that she is able to choose them.

What happened over the next few weeks was very interesting. Katie spent more time with her full-fat friends and less time with the others. She stuck up for herself more and even told her friends when they did something she did not like. Katie seemed happier and she appeared to be easing her pattern of fleeting friendships in favour of just spending time with her two new best friends, even having occasional sleepovers. Katie had made a choice about who she wanted to spend most of her time with based on what was important to her.

If your teenager is having problems in telling her friends when to stop something she does not like, first ask her for her suggestions and then help her to come to her own solutions. If you are both stuck, then this system can help.

Speak to the friend in private and tell them these things:

1. What they did
2. Why it upset you
3. What you would prefer.

For example: 'Natalie, it really upsets me when you speak about people behind their backs. I wouldn't like to be spoken about behind my back so please don't do it about others in front of me.'

Notice how it is all 'I'. At no point did we make Natalie wrong. Your teenager must also be ready for whatever reaction Natalie may show. In my experience most friends will just apologize. Some will not take the news so well. You then need to have a conversation about how you will both handle it if that happens.

2. The way she sees herself

This is always a difficult one as teenage girls are bombarded with images these days that are enough to make even the most self-assured person a little insecure. Even JK Rowling has revealed that she is constantly worried her daughters will grow up to be 'empty-headed, self-obsessed, emaciated clones'. So if you are worried about this, as a parent you are not alone!

I gave Louise three suggestions to try out:

1. When Katie looks at images in a magazine or newspaper, ask her what she thinks about them and how they make her feel. So when there is a picture of a perfect Paris Hilton, ask her how she feels and what she thinks of Paris and her exploits, and how she thinks Paris may feel about herself.
2. When Katie criticizes part of herself, ask her why she thinks that way and what you can do about it together.
3. Each day, point out at least one thing about her that is good; relate what you say to internal qualities as well as to what is visible from the outside. In this way she will learn that there is more to her than what is just on the outside.

It can be difficult for parents to raise the self-esteem of teenage girls in a world where materialism and looking good appear to be top priorities. Question your own and your daughter's ideas of perfection and what they mean. When she says something about a celebrity or someone else she sees, or even makes an awful comment about someone you pass in the street, challenge her. Challenge her to look inside and look beyond how someone appears, help her to understand that there is no such thing as perfection. Also, acknowledge that caring how you feel can be a good thing and can boost self-esteem. Help her as much as you can to feel and look good on the inside as well as on the outside.

Louise and Katie had some fruitful conversations. They realized that Katie was not always making the best out of the way she looked. Often, by wearing the wrong clothes she looked 'bigger' than she was. They went shopping together and bought clothes that made her feel good. Louise realized that Katie really thought nothing of the models who bared all for stardom. She actually cared more about what she called 'natural beauty'. She felt the pressure to look good. They talked about how modern expectations related to natural beauty and what signs she wanted to give out; what she wanted people to think about her when they looked at her. Katie began to learn that there was much more to her than met the eye. She appreciated the calmness that she brought to situations, the different perspective that she added and the fact that she wanted people to see her in a positive light. Over the next few months Louise and Katie began to make more sense of Katie's style and how she wanted to portray herself. Katie walked differently and felt better about herself.

 TIME OUT ···

We have to acknowledge fashion trends but we can help our teenager to feel more respect for herself at the same time. When your daughter comments on what someone is wearing, be it good or bad, you can ask what image she thinks it gives out, what it says about the person wearing it. When she is wearing something that may give a certain impression, ask her what she thinks people will think about her wearing it and if that is what she wants them to think. This way you get her to think about it without making her feel she is wrong.

....

3. Her fear of public transport and anything else that frightened her

Katie was showing signs of being more positive. Next, we had to deal with the fact that she seemed frightened of everything and relied too much on Louise to do things that ought to be very simple for a fourteen year old.

Life is partly about taking risks, and doing things that you find daunting. This is one of the ways in which we find out what we are capable of doing and is one of our biggest learning opportunities. When parents are over-protective and don't want their children to get hurt or to feel frightened, they sometimes over-compensate and do too much for them, even opting for the quiet life rather than listening to a teenager whining.

This is what Louise had been doing. When Katie did not want to do something such as going on the tube or going to the corner shop on her own, Louise had given in and done these things for her, often picking her up in the car from a friend's house when a tube station was close by or going to the shop to get something she wanted. Louise just could not cope with the tantrums and whining that Katie went into so she just gave in. Louise and I talked about it and established that Louise was not afraid of what would happen to Katie, she was just giving in to keep the peace. I asked Louise, 'If you keep giving into her, what might the consequence be?' Louise was quick to answer, 'She will never learn to take care of herself and I don't want that!' Louise realized that if she was saying 'yes' so often to Katie she was also saying 'no' to herself and giving up her time to do what she wanted to do. Thinking of time as a bank account and realizing that if she took some out for Katie she was decreasing her own balance, which would eventually go into the red, helped her to come to the same conclusion I did. It needed to stop and it needed to stop soon.

So we devised a simple system. When Katie asked her to do something that she was too scared of herself, like going to the shop or going on the tube, Louise was to follow this method:

1. State firmly, 'No, I am not willing to do that.'
2. Ask how she could help Katie to do it.
3. Stay calm and focused and continue to repeat what she had said previously while Katie whined and did whatever she did.

This was all she needed to do and she needed to do it consistently. I sensed that it would be difficult for Louise not to give in to Katie. Louise stayed true to her word. She refused to give Katie lifts, or to go to the shops, if these were things Katie could reasonably do herself. All that appeared to happen was that Katie gave up, went to her room and didn't get what she wanted. After about three weeks, Katie needed a certain pen to do her homework and since she was so particular about getting her schoolwork right this was a real opportunity for Louise.

Louise followed the system and this time, instead of Katie going up to her room she asked her mum two things:

1. Could she borrow her mum's mobile phone while she went to the shops?
2. Could Louise wait at the front door for her?

Louise agreed and for the first time ever Katie went to the shops alone. She came back very pleased with herself, although looking a little flustered. Gradually, Katie did more things by herself, even getting on the tube a few times to travel a few stops to her friend's house. Then crunch day came when Katie decided that she wanted to go into town which was ten tube stops away. This route would be much busier than the few stops she was used to travelling. Louise agreed as she was going with some very sensible girls.

At 3pm Louise got a very stressed phone call from Katie. She had lost her friends, was at the tube station and wanted to be picked up. It was very obvious that Katie was scared and feeling very uncomfortable with the situation.

FREEZE: WHAT WOULD YOU HAVE DONE? ·········
Would you have told her to stop being so silly, gone to pick her up right away, or just told her to get on with it?

Louise was tempted to pick her up but she didn't. She calmly stuck to the system and told her she could not. They talked about it and Louise suggested a way that made Katie feel safer. Katie agreed to do it – she had to find some passengers that she felt safe with. She wanted to find a lady with a push-chair and a lady in a suit, who were sitting in one of the busiest compartments. After letting five tube trains pass she did find people that fitted the bill. When they got off the train, if she did not feel comfortable in the carriage she either got into another compartment or waited for another train. This forty-minute journey took her two hours to complete but the point was that she did it and Louise had not stepped in. A small victory had been achieved!

4. The way she dealt with her sensitivity

The more confident and self-assured Katie became, the less this was a problem, but sometimes she was badly affected by comments from other people so we decided to put a system in place. We had to acknowledge how she felt while also getting her to take responsibility for her feelings.

When Katie was hurt by what someone said this is what Louise needed to do.

First, she needed to acknowledge that she was hurt: 'Katie, I can see you are hurt and that what has happened has affected you.'

Secondly, she was to ask her what she needed right now. Was it to be alone, to be hugged, to talk, what was it? Then she had to carry it out.

Thirdly, she was to let her know that when she wanted to talk, she would be there to listen. The whole point was not to push anything but to wait for Katie to come forward. When she did want to speak, Louise was to ask her the following questions:

1. How did what happened make you feel?
2. What could you have done about it to make yourself feel better?
3. What did you learn?
4. What would you do differently next time?

You could use this system at home with your child quite easily. The main thing is to make every instance a learning opportunity.

Louise used this system when she needed to and Katie moved forward in leaps and bounds. She certainly feels better about herself and looks like a different person. She still gets frightened but she just gets through it. I asked Louise what she had learnt most from the experiences and she said, 'Katie is her own person, she can be confident and self-assured in her own way and that is what I need to get used to.' Hear! Hear!

Action Points

1. Problems versus personality

Take a look now at all the things you think your teenager needs to work at. Be honest with yourself and ask, 'Which of these are problems and which may be due to her personality?' Which are the personality traits in her that you may be trying to 'fix' but that don't need fixing? How could you begin to see these personality traits as good qualities; how may they help her?

2. Self-Sense

Start to help your teenager to find a sense of herself. Take every opportunity you can to help her work out what she really wants, why she feels the way she does and what she can do about it.

3. Be curious.

Be very curious about why your teenager says and does the things she does. Go investigating and don't accept anything but the whole truth. When she acts a certain way or says a certain thing, ask yourself why you think she does that, what may be her reason and then ask everything you can as a possible exploration.

4. Everything is an opportunity.

Use every opportunity you can to talk to your teenager about self-image and the characteristics of successful teenagers, for example, pictures in magazines, on the TV, people in the street. Speak with her and ask her what her thoughts are, what she thinks of current trends and the behaviour of some of the role models being shown by the media.

5. Build her up.

When your daughter knocks herself down, build her up. Don't let her accept the low opinion of herself.

6. Challenge her.

Don't be afraid to challenge your daughter when you think she does not feel very good about herself. Every week think of a way you can help your daughter to think differently or do something different. A sure-fire way to increase someone's confidence is by getting them to do something they are scared of.

12

The A to Z Guide – first-aid kit for parents of teenagers

Parents are often in situations which they feel are hopeless and unchangeable. I want to give you something that you can turn to quickly when desperate. Something that will help you think, change your perspective and give you hope. The First-Aid Kit will help you do this. When you have a challenge with your teenager, turn to this section and look up the word which applies to your situation. The words and explanations are designed to start the healing process, to get you to take some action that will alleviate the problem a little, starting the relationship between you and your teen on the road to recovery. Some of these words will be familiar to you and will be found throughout the book. Others will be new. Some of them are light and a bit of a laugh; some are deadly serious. Only you can know which one of these words is most appropriate for your situation and circumstances. They are not supposed to be the full cure, but to give you a little hope, help you make a small step forward, change your thinking a little and show you that, whatever the situation, you can take action.

A

A is for affection, agreements and appreciation

Affection

It seems sad to me that I have to even mention this, but for those of you who have watched my TV series, you will know that there are times when parents just cannot show affection. When our teenagers are being difficult and making our lives a misery, it can be hard for us to show them any affection. People need affection to feel loved, cared for and happy. If teenagers don't get your affection, they will find ways to get your attention, which may not always be positive! Never underestimate the power of a hug!

Agreements

I know you have found me using this many times and I did consider whether I should repeat it here. To be honest, though, this is so important that to have left it out would have been foolish. Agreements alone can solve many problems in a less than harmonious household.

I think we live in a world that is all about winning, getting one over on another person and being right. There appears to be little room for compromise, understanding and agreement. Nowhere to me does this seem to be more relevant than in the relationships with our children. 'Because I told you so!' is a phrase frequently used and I often hear parents use the words 'battle', 'win' and 'enemy' when they refer to their teenagers. It really worries me. We are not at war with our teenagers (although it may feel like that); we are just living with someone who has a different point of view from our own and who may not always do as we say all the time. Is that really a bad thing?

Inevitably, when we live in close proximity with other people, there are bound to be times when we all get a little fraught with each other. However, in these moments is it right for us to say, 'You know what, I am the adult and you will do as I say'? Do we really have the right to control another person? Would it not be more productive to think about how the family, as a team, can agree on something that makes everyone feel better? This kind of thinking will move your relationship forward, keeping the lines of communication open, teaching your teenager a valuable lesson that life is not really about controlling others, it is about negotiating and reaching a compromise.

There are three steps in making agreements with your teenagers. If you want to be reminded of them, go back to Chapter Two, which is about responsibility.

Appreciation

A word for me that is not used enough in our daily life. We take for granted so many things, especially our children. Despite the fact that sometimes they drive us mad and make our lives a misery, they can also fill us with joy and happiness and do so many small things for us that go unnoticed and unrecognized. I believe that every day we should tell the people we love what we are thankful or grateful for, whether it was the fact that they fed the cat without being asked, put their school bag in its proper place or made you a cup of tea. We need to say thank you more often. I remember once watching a family on a TV programme. I counted up that the son, during one day, had made his mother about twenty cups of tea. Not once had she said thank you. Amazing! Here is the key: if your teenager feels he is appreciated, then he will do more for you. You will begin to see more of the behaviour that you can appreciate. If you make me twenty cups of tea a day and I don't say thank you once, what are you thinking? Each day, say thank you at least once to your teenager and start to notice all the things they do for you. Believe me, there will be something good that even the most hardened teenage alien does every day!

B

B is for boundaries

This is also a concept that I have introduced into the book on a few occasions and really goes hand in hand with agreements. You make agreements about the boundaries in the house. I prefer to use the word 'boundary' instead of 'rule'; to me a rule is a very rigid word and promotes ideas of authority and regulations and will send any teenager, or adult for that matter, into rebellion. It is natural behaviour for us to want to break the rules that someone else has imposed on us; we only have to look at the title of Marcus Buckingham and Curt Coffman's book, *First Break all the Rules*, to know this is true of everyone. No one likes rules! A boundary to me is much more flexible and is an indication of the furthest limit that a person is prepared to go. It gives a teenager a limit to his behaviour rather than a rule to stick to. Boundaries can be negotiated and agreed, rules are just set and adhered to. If you want cooperation from your teenagers then work with boundaries, not rules. Here is a little tip for you when agreeing boundaries – always offer up a boundary that is not your final limit; teenagers like to negotiate and will always push the boundaries a little. For example, if you want to set 10.30 as a time to come in, start negotiating at 9.30, be prepared to agree at about 10.00 and then be prepared to stretch it to 10.30. What this means is that your teenager will think he has won by making you agree to 10.00. He will then push it a little further and be ten minutes late, just because that is what a teenager does, but really you have won because you wanted 10.30. So you both have got what you want and it will be our little secret! You need to be prepared to be a little flexible and remember that although it may feel as if your teenager has one over on you, actually, he hasn't. If, however, he does stretch the time and comes in past 10.30, then you would need to step in, stating that it was unacceptable and then impose a remedy or penalty. It is a very clever way of stopping conflicts while also getting what you want.

I suggest that parents set boundaries covering these five areas.

1. Eating
2. Sleeping
3. Responsibilities – including jobs and chores
4. Money
5. Behaviour.

Be prepared to discuss these with your teenagers and negotiate agreements on each one.

C

C is for choice, commitment, consequences and consistency

Choice

I am a big believer in choice, what it promotes and the results it generates. As adults we are faced with choices every day, yet often we do not allow our children the same privilege, telling them where and when they must do something, in our efforts to control them. Recently, I was working with a twelve-year-old who refused to go to school and had not been there for seven months. Her family, very concerned, just kept telling her she had to go and the more they told her, the more she dug her heels in. I asked her what her choices were in this situation; she stated that staying at home was her only choice. I then asked her what other choices there were and together we drew up a list of four other choices – on-line school, home tutoring, going back to her old school or picking a new school. She initially opted for the on-line school and within a week we had her learning again. Every time she asked me what I thought she should do, I just told her that the choice was hers and that I trusted her to do what was right. After a month she said she was ready to go back to her old school. Now, she has successfully spent a week back at school. The point is, the pressure was taken off her and the rest of the family and she was able to make a choice by herself. She did what was right. When you are struggling with one of your teenager's issues, go through the choices with him, tell him the choice is his and that you trust him to do what is right. Then watch him squirm. He will find this concept difficult, since he is so used to being told what to do and having something to fight against, that he is not sure what to do. Most teenagers in this situation will eventually make a good choice. You just need to get off his back and allow him the time.

There are a few other ways you can use this tool. Instead of saying, 'Tom, go and do the washing up now!' you can say, 'Tom, you can do the washing up now or after this TV programme, which do you choose?' You are giving him choice but also making sure that what needs to be done gets done.

I have also, throughout the book, introduced you to the Choice and State technique which you can read more about in the Respect chapter.

'Tom, your dinner will be on the table in five minutes. You can come down now or later. However, I will not heat it up or cook you anything else later. The choice is yours.'

Whenever you are in any conflict with your teenager, work out a way to give him a choice which will ensure that what needs to be done gets done. Just think what a valuable lesson in life you are teaching him.

Commitment

I believe that commitment is important when bringing up a teenager: it is important for you as the parent to stay committed to your word, and also for the teenager to learn how to be committed. When a teenager makes a commitment to you or makes an agreement with you, you must not accept any excuse for him not following through. A teenager learns about maturity and worthiness by sticking to the commitments he has made. A parent who cares does not accept excuses. No excuse is acceptable for breaking a commitment and the resulting consequence may have to be followed by a remedy or a penalty. A parent who cares also stays committed to the teenager. As a parent, you must never give up on him, because if you do then he may give up on himself. So many parents tell me that they have given up and it infuriates me! How can you give up on your children? What they are really telling me is that it is too difficult and they don't know what else to do. In my estimation, that ought not to be used as an excuse to become uncommitted to your teenager. This is how I can succeed where some parents fail. I have developed my skills in working with teenagers over a long period of time, but most importantly I never give up. I believe that whatever has happened in the past, children can succeed and can learn to be responsible for themselves. I stay committed, no matter what. There can never be an excuse to give up, for your teenager or for yourself!

Consequences

Every action has a reaction and everything your teenager does will have a consequence, good or bad. What you need to ensure is that when an agreement is broken, the consequence that follows is one from which your teenager can learn and grow. Not just a spur of the moment, 'I am going to take your TV away' kind of thing. What most parents will resort to is a punishment. If a teenager does not conform, they tell the teenager what is wrong and then tell him that if he does not stop, he will be punished. The parent will make the judgement and enforce the punishment. Punishment takes responsibility away from the teenager and does not allow a better course of action, which is to offer a choice. William Glasser describes punishment as a '... gun being pointed at a teenager's head to motivate him'. He goes on to say that this is ineffective as the teenager will only conform while the gun is pointed at him. When it is lowered, the motivation to do the right thing goes away. Even worse, he becomes so used to the fear of the gun that it is no longer effective. All punishment does is teach a teenager to conform rather than to think and take responsibility for himself.

I suggest that you take your time to think of the consequences and give yourself at least twenty-four hours before discussing anything with your teenager. For example, a broken agreement relating to getting-up time will have a natural consequence – lateness for school. Always think about what you are trying to teach your teenager and respond from there. For example, if you are trying to teach him about responsibility, then the consequences of any action, together with any subsequent penalties or remedies, have to be related to responsibility. There is more on this topic in Chapter Two on responsibility and in Chapter Eight, My teenager thinks he is the boss.

Consistency

Consistency is about sticking to what you have agreed with firmness. This is twofold: what you have agreed with your teenager (including any consequences) and what you have agreed with yourself (for example, 'I will no longer rescue them'). To get anywhere with your teenager and to implement any plan, you will need to be consistent, and to be consistent you need perseverance, persistence and a lot of patience.

'But I've tried it and it didn't work!' is a statement I hear so often from parents and when I dig deeper, what it boils down to is that they tried it two, maybe three times and they didn't get the results they wanted, so they gave up. To get results, you need to stick to the plan and use the tools again and again with a degree of firmness and discipline. Some of these tools you may need to use one hundred times before you see a breakthrough, some you may only need to use once. Each situation, each teenager and each parent is different, and while I cannot guarantee that you will get instant results every time, what I can guarantee is that if you give in, you will see no results. I know how challenging it can be and I know how easy it is to give in and give up, but persistence and patience are key here. The founder of Kentucky Fried Chicken had to go to over 2000 restaurants before anyone would even taste his chicken, and Walt Disney went to over 360 banks before anyone would give him the money to start Disney World. What would have happened if they had given up after only trying twice? Any successful person will tell you that success is down to one per cent inspiration and ninety-nine per cent perspiration! I have given you the one per cent inspiration, now you need to put in the perspiration yourself. Only by doing these things over and over again with the same discipline each time will you get results. So just before you send me an email telling me that you tried it and it didn't work, just think to yourself, 'Have I really tried enough? Have I really given it a chance?'

D

D is for discipline

One of the people who helped me put this book together and really make sense of my garbled words called me and told me that one word was missing from my book. That word was 'discipline'. It sent me into a spin! I hate the word. It conjures up so many negative feelings for me, perhaps to do with my police officer background or perhaps due to the fact that as a child I was always told that I needed 'discipline'. Or maybe it's because so many parents tell me that their child needs 'discipline' when really what they mean is that they want their child to do exactly what they say. As the conversation continued, this person asked me one simple question, 'Are you scared of this word?' I thought about it and realized that perhaps I was, and I could not let my feelings get in the way of the book I was producing. On looking up the word in the dictionary, I found it meant something different from what I had expected. The Collins Concise Dictionary defines 'discipline' as:

1 Training or conditions imposed for the improvement of [...] self-control, etc 2 Systematic training in obedience 3 The state of improved

behaviour etc, resulting from such training [...] 5 A system of rules for behaviour, etc 6 A branch of learning or instruction [...]

When I saw this definition, I could not disagree that in fact the whole book was about discipline, about training parents, about their own self-control and issuing instructions, about how to help teenagers to learn self-control. Indeed, I do expect that if you use this training and instruction, then behaviour will improve. It was there in black and white: I was talking about discipline – a disciplined approach that parents can use for their own self-control and to improve their teenager's behaviour. That is what you are doing: you are training your teenager and showing her how to be self-controlled and yet more importantly than that, you are learning a disciplined approach so you can apply this training with self-control. A disciplined approach helps our teenagers to commit to better decisions. So when things are challenging and perhaps not going exactly as you would have hoped, ask yourself if you are really disciplined in what you are doing. Is there something you can do about your own self-control? There is no way you are going to be able to teach it if you cannot practise it yourself!

E
E is for ease and easy

We parents can sometimes put so much pressure on ourselves that it is unbelievable. This pressure often manifests itself by us nagging our teenagers and dealing with our own feelings of embarrassment.

I have one thing to say to you. Ease up! Ease up on yourself and with your teenagers. We can make things so difficult for ourselves, always worrying and being anxious. Sometimes, if we tell ourselves that just for today, for the next hour or even the next five minutes we are going to ease off, then we can find ourselves feeling less burdened, relieving the pressure and tension. We have a choice: we can choose between the difficult way or the easy way. I am not saying that parenting a teenager is easy – anything but – I am saying that you have a choice if you want to take the pressure off.

In Robin Sharma's book *Family Wisdom from the Monk who Sold his Ferrari*, he mentions a technique that really hit home with me. He states that parents are leaders – leaders of their children – and they need to choose not what is easy, but what is right. Being at ease and doing the easy thing are completely different – the easy option does not require any effort. Suppose your child asks for £10: the easy option is to give it. The right option may be to tell him that he has had his allowance and you are not prepared to do that. Now when I say 'right', I do not mean that there is a 'right' or a 'wrong' way, just that there is a 'right' option for you and your family. If you don't give the £10, then the chances are you may get a slammed door, a few choice words and a teenage 'strop', but as long as you choose not to take that personally, remembering that what you did is right, then in the long run you will get the answer. It is right that your teenager understands the value of money and the fact that money is not just handed out. It is not right that they use you as a 'hole in the wall'.

So when you get the chance, do what is right and not what is easy, remind yourself that the teenage 'strop' is not your fault, just the choice that they have made. Ease up on yourself!

F
F is for fun

Think about it: what do teenagers bring to the world, if not fun? They know how to have a good time and live in the moment. As adults, there is a lot we can learn from that. Put a bit of fun back into your relationship and communicate with your teenager at her level. So often, every time parents talk to their teenagers, it is either to tell them off, to discuss their future, or about some other thing they are not doing in the way their parents would wish. They never appear to have small talk, to laugh or chat about anything that is fun. Use the moments you have with them to have conversations that don't make them wrong but are light and above all include an element of fun. Doing fun things together is, I think, imperative for any family, but don't just judge this by your idea of fun – as we have learnt in some case studies, what you think is fun may be your teenager's idea of hell! Ask him what he would like to do and accommodate that. Give your teenager the job of social secretary in the house and let him organize the things you all do together, with some guidelines, of course.

G
G is for guidelines

A lot of the time we really do set our children up to fail. We give them a job to do or agree on what chores they will be responsible for and then chastise them when they don't deliver to our standards. So what is missing, where did it all go wrong? Well, quite simply, you didn't give them any guidelines. Imagine that you go into an office one day and in front of you are some papers and envelopes. You are told that your job is to put the papers in the envelopes. You do as asked and after completing the job you proudly announce that you have finished, only to be told that the paper is in the wrong way and they needed four pages in each envelope. How are you feeling? Pretty angry I guess, and you want to scream, 'Why didn't you tell me then?' This is exactly my point. You cannot blame your child for a job badly done if you have not told them how. You have to be very specific. Just saying that the bathroom has to be cleaned is not enough. You may need to make a checklist of what cleaning the bathroom entails; guidelines to help complete the job. Just think of the word 'guidance' and what it means – leadership, instruction and direction. All too often, this is where parents slip up. If you are teaching your child about money and he has a certain amount each week, then you need to give him guidelines about what that money is for, how long it is meant to last and what happens when it runs out. If your child wants a friend to come over, you need guidelines. Don't expect your teenager to read your mind (yes, these aliens have incredible power, but it does not stretch that far!) or work it out for themselves. You need to tell them. Most arguments in the house can be prevented with a little bit of guidance from you.

H

H is for hear and help

Hear

I put this one in because we may think we listen to our teenagers a lot, but do we really hear what they say? Do we really give them the experience of being listened to? Do we sit down, shut up and really listen to them? Do we listen without judgement? Do we listen without interfering and trying to solve? Do we let go of our expectations and wants and truly, truly listen? Do we give them a fair hearing? Even guilty people are entitled to a fair hearing in a court of law, yet quite often we do not afford our children the same right. We jump to all sorts of conclusions without even giving them a fair chance to be heard. Doesn't everyone deserve that at least? So, next time your teenager speaks to you, listen and truly hear before you condemn her. Next time, give her a fair hearing! We have all experienced what it feels like to be truly listened to, so give her that experience.

Help

I have put this in here because I think it is important to discuss. I think there is a fine line between help, support and rescue. You will need to do all three with your teenager at some point, there is no doubt about that, but what you need to be doing more is offering help or support. Your teenager will learn nothing from you rescuing them but they may learn a lot from a supportive, helping hand. Be careful in your language with your teenager. To offer help implies that you are prepared to carry the burden in some way; to offer support implies that you are prepared to give aid and encourage, but not necessarily take on the burden of any responsibility. There will be times when you have to take on some responsibility, especially when it comes to financial matters. There will be times when your teenager requires more support, for instance when they are having relationship difficulties. So before you ask them how you can help, ask yourself if this is the most appropriate question, as it may mean you end up with some of the burden. Could it have been more appropriate to have asked what support was needed?

I

I is for initiate and initiative

I have included these because I think that a lot of problems can be sorted by just taking action, whatever it is. I often hear parents saying they are stuck and don't know what to do, and consequently they don't do anything. Just using your initiative and making an initial move can start you on the road. Doing nothing will certainly keep you where you are. Sometimes, you just need to ask yourself what you can do, what first step you can take, and then just do it. Get into a 'can do' attitude and just do something. Action creates initiative and before you know, you will have begun to improve the situation.

J

J is for 'Jim Dandy to the rescue' and judgement

Jim Dandy to the Rescue

Okay, so most likely you are asking, 'Who is Jim Dandy?' Let me explain: I love 1950s music and 'Jim Dandy to the Rescue' is a great song by LaVern Baker. This song always makes me laugh as it depicts a man who runs around saving women.

Jim Dandy on a mountain top, 30,000 feet to drop, spied a lady on a runaway horse, uh-huh, that's right of course! Jim Dandy in a submarine, got a message from a mermaid queen, she was hanging from a fishing line, Jim Dandy didn't waste no time!

It reminds me of how most of us want to be rescued. We believe that there is a Jim Dandy out there. When it comes to relationships with your teenagers, there is no such thing. No one will be there to rescue you, there is no miracle cure, you have to do it yourself. While we are on the subject of rescue let me also point out that it is not your job to rescue your teenagers either. They will get themselves into uncomfortable situations and some may even be a little risky, but unless they are in real danger it is not your job to rescue them. So think twice before running to their aid and instead, ask them how they can get themselves out of the situation. Don't just run and pick them up when they call because they spent the taxi fare, encourage them to get a taxi home and then deduct the cost from next week's allowance; they may think twice about spending that taxi fare again. Don't be a Jim Dandy to your kids!

Judgement

There is a difference between judging and using your judgement. While I certainly do not want you to judge your teenager, I do want you to use your judgement. If you look up the word 'judgement' in a dictionary, it is described as the faculty of being able to make critical decisions and achieve a balanced viewpoint. If you could offer your teenager decisions made from a balanced viewpoint, then what more could he ask for? So before you make any decisions about your teenager, make sure that you have all the information and opinions you need to get a balanced viewpoint. Don't make rash judgements, and take the time to consider all the options.

K
K is for kind

I remember reading a particular book (although I've forgotten the title!) when this quote jumped out at me: 'When you have a choice to be right or kind, be kind.' This statement had such a profound effect on me. I thought I was always right and I had to win, come what may. I think doing the right thing is different from having to be right, so don't get the two confused here. The thought that I could choose had a powerful effect on me and suddenly, I began to realize that I was indeed in charge of myself in every situation. So now, if I am having a conversation with one of my children and I know for certain that I am right about something and they are wrong, I just sit there and remember that I can choose to be kind. I agree with her that she is right and let the situation go. It takes a lot of courage as a parent to do this, and letting go of something when you know you are right is a difficult thing to do, but with it comes incredible freedom. We are against everything in the world, it is so hard for us to give in and be kind. Don't get me wrong, I am not talking about giving in on very important things, just the minor everyday things. So if your teenager insists that you are having sausages again for the third night in a row, which you know is not true, just agree. Really, it is quite fun and stops arguments dead in their tracks. When your teenager spouts an opinion about something, instead of telling him he is wrong and shouldn't think like that, tell him his viewpoint is interesting, but that you believe something different. Sometimes, really arguing over the fact that the school bag is not put back in the right place is not worth it. Just be kind and put it there yourself. Don't make everything a right and wrong situation; just being kind can be enough.

L

L is for learning, listen and love

Learning

Look at everything that does not go according to plan in your home as a learning opportunity. Rather than seeing failure and disobedience, see a situation to learn and grow from. Learning is gaining knowledge or acquiring a skill. Is that not what we are here for as parents, to impart knowledge and support our children to learn all the skills they require for life? Don't react to every situation. Instead, give yourself thinking time and ask yourself, 'What is the learning opportunity here? What do I want to teach my child?' Respond from there.

Listen

We have spoken about listening a lot in this book and how important it is to listen in the right way. In Chapter Four I introduced you to the 'Step into my Shoes' listening skills. Here, I am just going to go over that with you briefly.

Learning to listen from your teenager's point of view (what I call 'Step into my Shoes' listening) requires dedication and a lot of patience. When practising this type of listening you are trying to get inside your teenager's mind, to look at the situation through her eyes; you are stepping into her shoes, trying to understand her interpretation of the world, how it must feel to be a teenager in today's society with all the challenges that must bring.

'Step into my Shoes' listening is a three-step process. You can find this in detailed form in Chapter Four, page 68.

If this feels a little too challenging to start with, use the 'Listen and Respect' technique in Chapter Seven, page 120. This is a really easy technique to implement and the result can be very successful when used over long periods of time.

Love

Now I really didn't want this to be one of those books where I tell you that all you really need to do is love your teenager, but I feel I have to mention love somewhere. Even in the really bad times, if we can remember that we love him then often that is enough! We can remember the adorable baby we gave birth to and, despite what appears to be the alien invasion, we do still love this child. So before you shout and scream and condemn, ask yourself, does this behaviour arise out of love? If it doesn't, then stop and think how you could make it do so. Coming from love does not mean that you give in and allow your child to walk all over you. It means that what you do, you do with an open heart, out of your desire to help your child become an adult. It means you don't do things out of hate, anger or revenge. It means that everything you do moves a situation forward and allows you to remain close to your child, while also offering learning opportunities.

M
M is for money, of course

During this book I introduced you to the Money for Chores system, so let's go through that again.

After helping parents and teenagers with countless systems about responsibility in the home, I have found the most effective ones with teenagers involve money. There are two advantages. First, you have them interested since you are talking about money. Secondly, you are teaching them the importance of managing and earning money. I call this system 'Money for Chores' and it is very easy to manage. Take the amount that you normally give your teenager for pocket money and divide it by four. Give her one quarter of the amount to start with. She can do what she wishes with it, it cannot be taken away for failure to do jobs or for bad behaviour. It is hers to keep. The other three quarters she has to earn by doing a number of jobs, which are worth a certain agreed amount of money each.

If you want to remind yourself of this tool again then read pages 36–7 in Chapter Two on responsibility.

N
N is for No, No, No

I have so many parents asking me what they can do about the fact that their children say 'No' to everything they say. The answer is simple. Stop asking questions that require a 'No' or 'Yes' answer. It sounds easy and really it is. There are two ways to do this. One is by offering choice as we did before – 'Are you going to put your school-bag away now or after this programme?' The other way is to use the 'I would like' method – 'It would be great if your schoolbag was away before dinner,' or, 'I would really like your schoolbag to be out of the way by the time we have dinner.' Can you see how both of them take away any resistance? Your teenager cannot say 'No' because you have not asked a question that allows a 'No' answer. If he fails to do what has been asked, you need to decide whether it is worth making an issue of it or not. You may decide to put the schoolbag away yourself and let him know you have done it. If this continues pick it up and throw it in the bin. He will soon get the message.

O

O is for opposite

I remember watching an episode of the *Simpsons* in which Homer had a parenting card in his pocket which said, 'Remember, whatever you want the boy to do, tell him the opposite.' This made me laugh as this kind of reverse-psychology *can* work. What I am asking you to do here is the opposite of what you would normally do. When we are stuck with a situation it can be really powerful for us to decide what we would normally do and then think about what the exact opposite would be. For example, if you normally nag your child as soon as he comes in about his homework, the opposite may be to not mention it, or to offer help if it is needed. I can assume that, because you have bought this book, your teenager is not a little angel and something is not working. So shock yourself and shock your teenager by doing the opposite of what you would normally do.

P
P is for penalties and personality

Penalties

I thought long and hard about this word before putting it in. In its broadest sense it does mean punishment, which is something that I don't agree with, since it does not promote learning. However, on further investigation I found that it also means loss or another unfortunate result of one's actions, which I do think fits with what we are talking about. If your child breaks an agreement or does something that is less than desirable, then there will probably be some kind of loss or unfortunate result. If we don't turn up for work, then we may get fired. If your child is late for school, she may get a detention. There is always some consequence that will be natural and this may be enough; however, sometimes you as a parent may also need to step in and issue a penalty. So this is how I want you to look at it: something happens and an agreement is broken, so there is a natural consequence. It is your job as a parent to decide whether you also need to issue a penalty. If your child was caught by the police, then a stint in the cells may be enough. However, if she is late for school a detention may not do the job. You then need to ask yourself, 'What is the remedy?' This is the first important step. If your child is late for school, the remedy may be that she can no longer set her own bedtime and that you set it for a few weeks. In order to do that you may have to issue a penalty by taking the TV and Play Station out of the room. You would only issue this penalty, however, if the first remedy had not worked. So think of this as a three-step process. I suggest that the first time this happens you let the natural consequence be enough, and only if it happens again do you move on. If it happens a second time, ask yourself what the remedy to this problem is, and impose it. If that does not work, then step in with a penalty. The very best thing to do is discuss this with your teenager, so that she gets a say and knows the score, but sometimes, you will just have to step in.

Personality

Every child is different, with a unique style, a unique way of handling situations and responding to others, a unique way of behaving and a unique way of thinking. Methods and techniques you use with one of your children may not work with the other one. Each child needs a separate approach. Understanding your teenager and her motivations is the first step in improving behaviour. The tool that I use for understanding personality types is the enneagram. Here again is an overview of that tool.

The enneagram identifies nine main personality types. While we each possess more than one of the nine types, we show preference to one more than the others. I find this tool extremely useful in helping teenagers to understand themselves and other people. See

Chapter Five on sibling rivalry for a full description of the nine personality types (pages 87–9).

Q
Q is for questions

Questions are the lifeblood of coaching and they can be the tool that moves you and your teenager forward too. We are not talking about any old question here, but what we in the coaching world call powerful questions; questions that move a person forward. Powerful questions are not accusatory – 'Why did you do that?' – neither are they to elicit information – 'What did she say next?' Powerful questions aid the person in thinking and learning. 'How did doing that make you feel?' 'What do you think you could have said that would have changed her mind?' Powerful questions nearly always begin with 'How' or 'What'. So next time you are frustrated with your teenager, sit down and ask yourself how you can move this situation forward with a What or How question.

R
R is for remedies, respect and responsibility

Remedies

Remedies are explained in great detail under Penalties as they do go hand in hand. A remedy is something that you put in place to 'cure' a constant challenge with your teenager. When your teenager does something wrong, instead of punishing him, first ask yourself, and then him, what the remedy is. At the end of the day I am assuming that you want the situation to improve. To do that you need to put a remedy in place first. So before you think anything, think remedy.

Respect

Gosh! I don't think I can go on about this enough. Respect is to hold someone in high esteem and regard, and don't we all deserve that? Even your little alien does. Distinguish in your mind between the things she does and who she is. She may behave badly but inside she is still a human being (honest!) who craves acknowledgement from the one person who means the most in the world to her – you! Ensure that you let your teenager know everyday that you respect who she is and the great qualities about her. However bad it gets and however desperate your situation becomes, just turning your mind to respect will help alleviate the problem.

Responsibility

This is one of my favourite subjects and any teenager who has worked with me gets sick of me saying, 'How can you take responsibility for yourself here?' and 'What part of this situation can you take responsibility for?' Whether we like it or not, we have responsibility in every minute of our day and this is what we need to teach our children. We are all accountable for our actions and our decisions and anything else is not important, as far as I am concerned. Support your child by always thinking about responsibility. Responsibility is learned through evaluating each situation and choosing a path that that person thinks will be more helpful for them. A child who has responsibility for his own evaluation learns to become more responsible. Irresponsible children don't know how to behave better.

The easiest way to teach your child responsibility is to always ask him if what he is doing is helping the situation and getting him what he wants, and then to help him to discover better choices that he can make. When he tells you that none of it was his fault and it isn't fair, question that – go further. When he blames someone else, remind him that no one person can control another and ask what he does take responsibility for. And as for, 'I have a right to do whatever I want!' – yes, he does and with every right comes a responsibility, so remind him of that. 'Yes, you may have the right to say whatever you wish, but you also have a responsibility to understand that what you say may hurt others.' Are you understanding this? It is very important!

S

S is for strategy and support

Strategy

You have read most of this book now and you are most probably aware that I believe a good strategy can put an end to most problems in your home. If we look at the word 'strategy', it means a long-term plan for success. Is that not what you want? Don't leave this tool for the sole use of business, it has as much use in the family as well. So think strategy and put one in place.

Support

Find some. What more can I say? Taming a teenager is no mean feat and it takes dedication, commitment and time. It is probably the most difficult job in the world. Don't take this job lightly. You need support for yourself, be it from a coach, a friend, your partner or a family member – make sure you have someone who you can turn to when things get too tough. Find someone who can help you carry the weight that is on your shoulders, someone who can give you aid and courage when you need it. Let this person know what you need and how you want to be supported. Is it just a hug, will it be a 'right then' kind of situation or do you need to be asked certain questions?

While I am on the subject, look at how you support your teenager. How do you give her aid and courage? Do you support her too little or do you step in too often? Do you support her in all areas of life – physically, mentally, spiritually, financially and intellectually – or do you only offer support in a few. Letting your teenager know that you will support her when she needs it is a very powerful thing and should not be confused with stepping in, rescuing or doing everything for her. That is very different. Support is given through love, only when needed and in the way that the person wants it.

T

T is for talk and truth

Talk

We don't talk with our teenagers enough. Talking can quite often put any situation right. Talking is different from telling; it is about having meaningful conversation and sometimes it does not have to have an end result. Talking can open up the lines of broken communication and can begin to solve problems. Don't make this a 'sit down, I need to talk to you' kind of thing. Instead, make sure each day that you talk to your teenager and yes, that means a conversation where he talks back; even if you just get a few grunts, it will do.

Truth

Always tell the truth to your teenagers, as it will help you in the long run. So many of us hide things and feel that we need to look 'perfect' in front of our teenagers. Tell the truth at all times. If you are at a loss as to what to do in a certain situation, tell them. If they are making you lose all hope, tell them. I don't mean blame them or burden them with your problems, just be truthful with them as much as you can be. By being truthful you will earn their trust and in return you will get truth from them. The dictionary definition is: 'the quality of being true, genuine, actual or factual', and I think that we must at all times give them the situation as it is. Only then can people make real and informed decisions about what they want to do.

U

U is for understanding

'Seek first to understand and then be understood,' (Steven Covey). I think never were any truer words spoken. As a parent, seek first to understand your teenager and what he is saying before you seek to be understood. When you understand you can learn from your teenager, you can judge the situation better and you can make more informed judgements. Through understanding you can reach mutual agreements and be more sympathetic and tolerant. To seek to understand is to seek to comprehend the essence of your teenager and why they do what they do. Isn't this the best gift you can give them?

V

V is for very large gin

It is not that I condone alcoholism, I just could not think of another 'V' and I think as parents we often complain about how our children are driving us to drink. Bringing up children is exhausting and takes so much energy and time that we do need to switch off and relax as much as possible. While the odd Chardonnay won't do you any harm, if this is your only way of dealing with stress you may be in trouble! So think of other ways to relieve the tension, other ways that you can take care of yourself and other ways you can ensure you have time to yourself. It is vital that you do this. Think of it as a bank account – you need to put in to take out and if all you do is take, take, take, then eventually you will get overdrawn!

W
W is for wishing and whining

Wishing and whining – my two pet hates. No amount of wishing is going to make your situation any better and no amount of whining is going to make your teenager do what you want him to do. These are victim behaviours, so stop them now! Having the want or desire for something to happen is not enough, you need to take action. 'I just wish he could think about his future.' 'I just wish he would do what I say.' 'I just wish, I just wish . . .' Stop, stop, stop! Wishes are for fairy tales and you are not in one. Wishing leaves you powerless and makes you negate responsibility. What will that teach your teenager?

X
X is for X-rated language

X-rated language! I cannot tell you how many parents have told me that they want their teenager to stop swearing. Only under further examination do they tell me that they themselves swear at home sometimes. I don't care if it is sometimes, once a week or every day, it has to stop. If you want your teenager to stop then you need to lead by example. Children mimic behaviour and if you want them to stop it, you stop it first. Only then are you in a position to tell him not to swear. You don't swear at him, so you don't expect this sort of behaviour from him. To my mind, if you cannot do that then really you don't have a leg to stand on.

Z
Z is for zzzzzzz . . .

And finally, sleep — so important. Sleep can cure a host of things and tired parents make bad, irritated and grumpy parents who find it very hard to parent effectively. If you want to be the best parent you can be and support your teenager in the best way possible, then you need to sleep — simple. Don't tell me that you have loads of things to do; so does every parent, so do I. If you don't make way for your sleep then you make way for other things. Let your family know that they need to support you and tell them how they can help to make sleep a priority. There is a reason people say sleep on it. Things do look better after a restful night.

13

The most common alien attitude invasions and what to do about them

In this chapter I want to have a bit of fun, while at the same time giving you some strategies for dealing with what I see as the most common forms of alien invasions. What do I mean by that? What I am referring to are the 'bad attitudes' that begin to appear and often take parents by surprise. What I have found is that these attitudes tend to start developing before the teenage years but generally go unnoticed, due to the fact that they are not really so intense. However, in the teenage years the intensity of these attitudes seems to escalate. A simple conversation or request can turn into intergalactic war! I will describe here the common attitude invasions I see and the strategies that I have used successfully with other parents.

The 'I am not going to do a thing you say' invasion

This invasion can be a difficult one to crack and you will need patience, commitment and one of those very large glasses of gin that I mention in the A–Z Guide. This attitude can be very intense and can lead to angry outbursts and constant battles if you are not careful.

So, what is this invasion all about? What your teenager is saying to you is, 'I am nearly an adult now and think I am independent. I don't want to be told what to do!' This is your teenager fighting for a piece of independence and the right to do things his way. While you may not agree with it and you may think, 'While you are still under my roof you have to do as I say,' you cannot stop it. Fighting against this, or any attempts to escape, will be futile.

This attitude is here to stay and you need to learn how to deal with it and tame it.

So let's look at the word 'independent'. It means being free from control and not dependent upon others, not relying on others for financial support, for example. Can you really see your teenager doing that? No, me neither.

So how do you deal with it? I think the best way is to face it running, to head it off at the pass and to talk to your teenager about it. When the moment is right, let him know that you understand that as he gets older, he wants more independence. Doing what others ask of him can be a real bind and you really want to help him to become independent. However, while he is still at home you all need to work together as a team, and that means all doing things that sometimes we don't really want to do. Ask him how he wants you to help him as he searches for independence, and ask him what you can do to make it easier. Also, tell him what you want and what you expect from him. Make agreements together about how you will both function now in these new roles.

The language you use with a teenager like this is critical. The way you spoke to your teenager before this invasion is unlikely to have the same effect now. You need to be very clear and concise. Are you asking him to do something or are you telling him? You need to be clear on these two so your teenager will know when he can negotiate and when he cannot. If you constantly ask everything, he will negotiate. If you tell him to do everything, then he will rebel. An 'ask' is generally about something unimportant and the teenager could say 'No' or do it later. A 'tell' has a sense of urgency about it and is something that must be carried out now.

So how does this work in practice? Let's say that Paul has come home from school and left his bag in the hall. It is not very important (other than the fact that it annoys you) so you could say, 'Paul, please can you put your schoolbag away?' The response may well be 'No', in which case you will then say, 'Paul, it is your responsibility to put your schoolbag away and I want it away before tea is on the table. Do you understand?'

If it is something more important, for example, you are about to go out and he needs to be in the car now, you would say, 'Paul, come downstairs now, we're leaving.' It is more of an order or instruction and if he doesn't respond, there is no second chance, you leave. Your tone in the use of these phrases is critical, too. An 'ask' is gentler but still has some firmness about it. A 'tell' is much more authoritative and demanding. When you start using 'ask' and 'tell' more effectively your teenager will gradually recognize the difference.

If the 'I am not doing anything you say' attitude continues after this, then it is time to bring out the big guns. Let your teenager know that you are finding it difficult and that despite every effort on your part, he still does not contribute to the household and refuses to do anything. Let him know that you feel it is time to rethink your contribution and commitment to him. If he believes that he is independent enough, then you will need to rethink a few things – money, paying his phone bill, for example. Let him know you are thinking about this and that you would like his thoughts on it. Give him a few days to think about what you have said and see if he produces any ideas or suggestions. If not, then come up with a plan, like refusing to pay his phone bill until he agrees to be more helpful. Let him know what it is and carry it out. When he begins to see that what he puts in is equal to what he gets out, then he may change his mind. Once he realizes that the more unhelpful he is the less he gets, he will soon decide to knock this attitude on the head, at least until the next time!

The 'whatever' invasion

This type of invasion drives me mad. Suddenly, you feel that you need a phrase book to deal with your own child; the sentences become grunts. 'Whatever' and 'bothered' become part of everyday language.

In my experience, 'whatever' is normally only spoken when a teenager knows you are right. She will not admit it because she may lose face. Strangely enough, it can be a different way of saying 'Yes'. If you ask her if she wants to come into town with you and the answer is 'Whatever', then it is likely to mean 'Yes'. The same response may be given when you ask why the washing up hasn't been done – a job that she is responsible for – and most likely means that she knows you are right, but she doesn't want to do it. So in some way, when you hear this word it can be a minor victory on your behalf. Allow yourself a celebration.

Any attempt to get your alien to use proper English or to explain to you what she means may well be met with hostility, so don't even try it! The more of an issue you make it, the more it will become her weapon of choice.

The best thing to do is to ignore the word itself and make it clear that you know what is meant by it. So when your child says, 'Whatever' to a request such as going into town, it can be met by you saying, 'I assume that means you want to go – if so, then I need you to be ready in fifteen minutes.' Or, in the washing up situation, 'I assume that means that you realize it is your responsibility and you know you should have done it by now. I want it done by nine o'clock.' By ignoring the word and stating what you believe it means, the word has less impact in your house. You just need to get over the fact that you find it disrespectful; it is, after all, only a word. Teenagers love to have a secret code and language, and you may just have to grin and bear it.

However, excessive use of this word may need more attention. Point out that you realize how it can often be frustrating and difficult to find the right words, but the use of 'whatever' will not help in improving matters. When she uses it again, ask her what she really wants to say to you.

You may never wipe 'whatever' completely off the map but you can give it a good run for its money.

The 'it's not fair' invasion

Doesn't this one just drive you mad? A 'life isn't fair' answer will certainly not tame these outbursts. What you have to do here is call their bluff.

Generally, claims of, 'It's not fair!' really mean, 'You are not giving me what I want! I am not getting what I want and I am angry and cross about it. I think you are not listening to me or understanding my point of view. That frustrates me and makes me think you are not being fair.'

So now you know what they really mean, you can do something about it.

The first option is to not let it even raise its ugly head.

Here is the common situation. The teenager asks for something like, 'Mum, can I go out tonight?' Without a second thought the parent says, 'No,' and the teenager storms out with a torrent of, 'It's not fair!' He could have a point, have you really listened to him? I heard someone say recently that if you look at the word 'listen', the last three letters are 'ten' and we should be listening ten times more than we are talking. So there is a lesson in itself.

The first thing to do is to listen and not trigger the behaviour. If your teenager asks you if he can go out or have friends over, just take a moment to think about the answer. If you want to say, 'No,' why do you want to say it? Is it because you are tired? Is it because you want to spend some time with him tonight? Is it because he keeps you up all night? What is it? When you are clear about the real reason, you can then move on. Instead of saying, 'No,' you are going to say, 'Yes,' but that does not mean that he has his own way. Here is how it works.

'I would love to have your friends over. However, I am really tired at the moment and when they are here you keep us awake all night. Let's look at doing it another night and see how this can work for everyone.' Do you see how I have taken the resistance away, and a 'not fair' is unlikely to come out? I have stated what I want and have offered a solution. Notice too that I did not use the word 'but'. I want you to take it out of your vocabulary when talking to your teenager. Use 'and' or 'however'; these words will move the situation forward more.

If you use this method, 'it's not fair' is unlikely to surface. You just need to carry on listening and attempting to find solutions that work for both of you.

However, if this does not work, or you don't take this route, you can always challenge what he is saying. If he says, 'It's not fair,' ask him what he thinks is unfair about the situation. Tell him that you are trying to understand his point of view and would really appreciate him sharing his concerns with you. You can even challenge him, asking if it was really what he wanted to say, or was he just frustrated at not getting his own way?

The key, as I stated before, is not to react, but to call his bluff. He will soon realize that 'it's not fair' is not getting him what he wants and he will eventually give it up as a bad job.

The 'you can't tell me what to do' invasion

On reflection, I think that nearly every teenager gets invaded by this one. It is one of the most annoying things that parents hear from their children's mouths. Your instant reaction is to say, 'Well, actually sonny, yes I can!' That will not get you anywhere!

Don't make this one a battle for power where one will win and one will lose. You may win, but the fight and journey along the way may lose you your relationship with your teenager. If this happens, then you are going to become less influential in her life and less likely to influence any future decisions.

So what do you do about it? You take some very deep breaths – easier said than done – and realize that your job is not actually to get your child to do what you want. It is to get her to grow up into an independent and responsible young adult.

Do not react to this comment. You need to challenge the thought process here and get her thinking. So responses such as, 'What makes you think that?' or, 'Tell me why you feel that way,' are useful. However, let's face it, you may not be able to use them in the heat of the moment.

The best thing is to say, 'I didn't mean to tell you what to do; what I meant to say is that you have a choice between this option and that option. Which do you choose?' Can you see how this takes the resistance away? You don't just say, 'You are wrong,' and clarify your point. Another way to do this is to say, 'You know what? I don't have a right to tell you what to do. However, I do have a right to let you know what I expect, so that you can then make a choice.'

Another option is to say, 'I may not have a right. However, I can say what is acceptable and unacceptable in my house. If you choose to do something unacceptable, then that gives me the right to choose what to do as a result.'

Can you see how all of these give the choice back to her and take the heat off you? Parenting is not about you being right and your child being wrong, so don't make it be that way. Who cares if they think you cannot tell them what to do? Really, after all, you know the truth.

The 'stay in bed all day' invasion

Oh, how annoying, in bed all day! Before you decide that he is just a lazy good-for-nothing, take heed of this advice.

Most parents find the sleeping habits of teenagers bizarre. They appear to become nocturnal in their activities. In Barbara Strauch's book, *Why are they so Weird?*, she explains in great detail the reason for such strange behaviour, from the change in melatonin levels to the fact that in the past, adolescents, as the most agile, had to stay up and be alert to defend the pack. Strauch believes that these in-built environmental qualities have lingered on and our teenagers find it difficult to go to sleep in the evenings because of this biological factor. She also stresses that research has shown that teenagers need nine hours' sleep; hence, they have an inability to go to sleep and an inability to get up, which is bound to lead to problems. Some schools in America have taken note of this and now start school hours later, but in Britain I think we have a long way to go yet! So maybe our teenagers are not lazy, just biologically impaired!

Sometimes, leaving them in bed can be the best option, as letting them catch up with their sleep can actually be a good thing. Teenagers need three hours of sleep more per night than adults and if they are not sleeping well throughout the week then this accumulates. If you can bear it, leave them in bed. What you need to decide, as a parent, is what is acceptable to you and what the guidelines are for them to stay in bed. Do you mind at all? Do you not mind as long as they get up by a certain time? Do you not mind as long as they spend some time with you? Or do you not mind as long as you don't have to force them out of bed on school days? Be very clear in your own mind about what the guidelines are and make sure your teenager understands them. Say something like, 'I know you need a lot of sleep and I want you to catch up on it. That is okay with me and I will leave you in bed. All I ask is that you get up in time to eat lunch with us.' Be clear about what you want and will accept as a family. You might also want to look at ways you can coax him from his cave. Cooking food he loves or doing something he finds exciting may be other ways that you can also beat this one. Shouting at him, telling him he is lazy and forcing him out of bed are just not going to work. If you do agree a cut-off time with him, then here are my suggestions for waking up your little darling without a slanging match.

- Go in at least an hour before he has to get up and open the curtains – natural light is a gentle way to bring someone around from a deep slumber.

- Get a very loud alarm clock and set it for thirty minutes before he has to get up. Put it in a place where he has to get out of bed to switch it off.
- If he is not up, go in five minutes before he has to be and in a stern authoritative voice, tell him it is time to get up.
- Do this two more times and then leave him to it.

On the last occasion tell him that you will not be coming in anymore.

Parents often ask me what to do if their children still do not get up. In all the time I have been using this technique this has only ever happened once, however if they choose to stay in bed after this point, then I recommend that you leave them in bed. If they lie in and are late for school, college or work, then under no circumstances write them a letter or help them out with a lift. It was their decision to stay in bed and they must face the consequences. When your child has been late for a few mornings and knows that you will not rescue them from their situation, they will start to take some personal responsibility for themselves. Parents who take their children to school in the car just because they got up late may never be able to win this battle. If the staying in bed continues after this, then it is time for the big guns! Remember, the lesson that your child must learn here is that they are showing a lack of personal responsibility. Think of other things for which they are responsible, perhaps their phone, or getting home by a certain time in the evening. When they ask you for more credit for their phone, to stay out late or to join a new sports club, remind them that they will need to take personal responsibility for these things and until they can prove to you that they can make good personal choices, for example, getting up in time, then you are not willing to give them more responsibility. When they know you mean business, they will begin to see the link between not getting up and taking personal responsibility. Believe me, this will have the desired affect.

A side note here is that making him go to bed early to get up early may not be a solution. Melatonin levels (which induce sleep) take effect much later with adolescents and sometimes will not peak until one or two in the morning. So even though he may go to bed, his pleas of, 'I can't get to sleep!' may actually be true. They are just not wired the same as we are when it comes to sleeping, so this invasion truly is one that they cannot control.

The 'treat the house like a hotel' invasion

This is something that I was often told when I was a child. I didn't understand it then and still don't! I used to tell my mum to stop doing things for me, so that I would have to do them myself – to me it was as simple as that. If you want your teenager to stop treating your house like a hotel, then stop allowing her to. This one is of your making, not hers. If someone cooked all your food and did all your washing and ironing, wouldn't you let them?

Be clear in your own mind about what you really mean in this situation – I find that parents often mean something entirely different, like they do not feel appreciated, respected or helped. Sometimes as parents we can even get jealous of the freedom and apparently easy life our teenagers have. Our thoughts are borne out of the frustration that we no longer have this freedom.

You don't have to do things for teenagers, they are capable of doing things for themselves. It does not make you a bad parent if they iron their own clothes or make their own food, should they choose not to eat with you. After all, are you not preparing them for life? Be clear about what you want and don't want to do for them and balance this out with the chores, if any, that they do around the house. If they contribute a lot around the house, you may do more for them. If they contribute less, expecting you to do everything, then what you do for them may be less. **You are not their slave, you are all in a family, working together as a team and that means you each do your fair share.** However, you cannot expect them to do things if they are not told or asked. Their brains simply do not work like that. If you want them to be responsible for their own washing then tell them, or if you want them to start ironing their clothes, show them how. What I absolutely do not want you to do is play the slave, do nothing about it, then whine like a victim. You are not a victim, you always have a choice. If they scream and shout because you will not do their ironing, then let them scream and shout. Don't give in; that is what they want you to do. However much they complain, tell them that this is your house, they are your children and this is how you are going to deal with it. They are just trying to hurt you in order to get you to do what they want.

Make a stand! Slavery has been abolished and if you are doing things for them that they could really do for themselves, stop it. If you are a parent who is prepared to do anything for a quiet life, then think of the price of that quiet life.

The 'jump down your throat' invasion

This is what I call the 'Walking on Eggshells phenomenon' and most parents tell me they suffer from it. They feel that everything they say is being taken the wrong way and that all their teenagers do is jump down their throat at every available opportunity. They get more and more frustrated and, in my experience, do one of three things. They can become silent, ignoring their teenager – not a good option since I am assuming that they do want a relationship with their teenagers; they may shout back, or they may become very sarcastic, which drives the teenager away even more. If what you want is some peace within your home, then none of these options will get it.

Your teenage alien may behave like this for a number of reasons. He may be worried or upset about something, he may want to get back at you for something he has not forgiven you for that happened weeks ago, or he knows that what you are saying is right and doesn't want to hear it.

So what do you do? What you don't do is react in any of the three ways I described above.

What I want you to do is follow a four-step system.

1. Point out the behaviour.
2. Be curious and investigate possible causes.
3. Tell him it is not acceptable.
4. Tell him what will happen if it continues.

So in practice if he shouts at you or jumps down your throat:

1. Say, 'Ben, do you realize you are shouting at me?'
2. Say, 'Is there anything worrying you or something you want to talk about?'
3. Tell him that it is not acceptable to shout at you and if he continues, you will leave the room.
4. If he continues then walk away.

Obviously, you will wait for your child to respond after each step. It may be that after step one the child apologizes and stops.

The system works for many reasons. It lets the child know what he is doing. Often, you do not realize you are doing something until it is pointed out to you. It puts you, as the parent, in control of the situation so that you don't have to react to what he is doing. You are teaching him that what he does and says has an effect on people. You are letting him know what is and is not acceptable and what the consequences of his actions will be.

You do not have to tolerate him shouting at you and jumping down your throat.

When you carry out this system you need to be focused, calm and collected, and to speak in a moderate tone. Shouting at him will not help the situation.

Don't get hurt by whatever is thrown back at you either, it is just him not knowing what to do or say. Remember, he is the child and you are the adult. As such, you should be the one to respond calmly. Only when you do this will your alien realize that perhaps what he is doing is not getting him the results he wants.

The 'silent treatment' invasion

The silent treatment – nothing worse, is there? You want to know what is going on, what the score is and he will not tell you a thing. If you are lucky, you may get a few groans and grunts, but that is all.

First, do not panic. Behaviour like this does not necessarily mean that your teenager has gone into some dark place, although if you are very worried then please take your child to a doctor. All it means is that your alien is hiding out in a cave for a while as she works something out. What we are dealing with here is a teenager who will not speak to you, not one who is down and appears to be depressed.

I find that in these situations the parents often give up, believing the silence to be insolence and a clear sign that the teenager does not want to be part of the family. Do not give up on a child like this. She still needs love and to know that you care. Don't restrict your conversation with her to what you get back in reply. Talk as you did before, still happy, jolly, inviting her to come along to things. Don't assume that silence means she does not want to take part. If she comes out of her cave and is miserable, don't have a go, give her time to respond. Making light of how she feels or making her feel she is in the wrong may only make the situation worse.

Comments like, 'If there is anything you want to speak about I am here for you. Come and speak to me if you want to,' will let your teenager know that you are there if she needs you.

Some teenagers may just be silent types, others may be thinking about their future and the tough decisions they are facing at the moment. Others may just not know what to say. Don't make an assumption about what it all means; keep her involved. If, however, the situation continues for months, then tell her you are worried and concerned for her. Tell her that you think she may need to speak to someone or see a doctor. Gauge her response. The best way is to allow her time to come to you for help.

If you are worried, take her to the doctor. In most cases this phase will pass and everyone will emerge unscathed. This invasion appears to be cured by time.

The 'out all night' invasion

A difficult one to crack. Having dealt with this on a number of occasions, I have found a link common to all cases. The teenagers have stayed out all night because they did not like being at home. Some felt they were always nagged, others felt that everyone told them how bad they were. Others could not stand the arguments, some were being picked on by siblings, some were being blamed for everything. Others stayed out because their parents sat in front of the TV all night and paid them no attention.

They stay out all night because they prefer to be somewhere else rather than with you. That is the real problem. I'm sorry to put it so bluntly and please don't be offended. There is a solution!

You have to be honest with yourself and ask why this is happening. Be brave and ask him why he stays out all night, why being at home feels so bad most of the time. He will be honest with you so be prepared, you may not like what you hear. That off-the-cuff comment you made four months ago about packing his bags for him when he reached sixteen may have been taken literally. When you know the reason you can then work on a solution and get him to help you implement it.

However, sometimes you may not know and he may not tell you, so here are some suggestions that you can use. One or all of them will have some kind of effect but there is no real substitute for asking them.

1. Have conversations with your teenager, however short, about things that do not appear as nagging or having a go.
2. Each day, thank your teenager for something he has done and tell him something you like about him.
3. Make your home a more pleasant place to be in, stop shouting and arguing. Who, given the option, would stay in a house like that?
4. Think before you lash out and blame – ask for his opinions and thoughts.
5. Just one night a week, do something that does not involve the TV, something he may like. Maybe go to the pictures, have a barbecue, something that he may want to join in with you. Don't make it compulsory, just an option. When he sees you having fun it will be hard to resist.

You may need to look at the agreements that you have made with your teenager about what time he has to come in, as well as the consequences if those agreements are broken. You can read more about this topic in Chapter Two on responsibility.

You may have to accept that you have a teenager who has lots of friends, is very social and just wants to go out and have fun. Staying at home with the boring parents may not be something that excites him as much as it did when he was small. He is growing up and his social circle may not involve you anymore. Get over it and have some fun yourself!

The 'care about no one but myself' invasion

Isn't this one just awful? This invasion doesn't normally happen because the teenager hates everyone else or doesn't really want to do things for others. More often than not it is simply a case of not thinking. That is what you need to get your teenager to do – think.

Don't fault her for being selfish, telling her what a bad person she is, because that is simply not true. Help her to link her actions with the feelings of others.

Suppose she makes herself a cup of tea and doesn't ask anyone else if they want one. Just say, 'Sam, I noticed you only made yourself a cup. How do you think that makes the rest of us feel?' Don't make her have to answer or make this a conversation, just pose the question. Whether you think so or not, your teenager will be processing this information. If she invites one friend to the pictures and not the other, ask her how she would feel if the tables were turned. Point out instances where people think of others and how other people give as well as receive. Speak with her about celebrities and how they give to charity. Look at your own way of behaving – can you be selfish sometimes?

Emphasize that you are all in a team and need to work together.

Don't respond by not involving her, as you are not teaching anything here. You can have a conversation about how she is making everyone else feel and how you love her and want her to be part of the family. Tell her that others are finding it difficult because it looks as if she does not care. When she does think of others, tell her how much you appreciate it and how good it made the other person feel.

Make it a normal practice that people share their things, that people ask before taking and that people also have the right to say, 'No'. Keep doing this and the selfishness will gradually disappear. Teenagers need to learn how to negotiate and cooperate with each other. For more information on this, please read Chapter Five on siblings fighting.

This invasion does tend to dwindle with age. As teenagers become more experienced and deal with more people, they begin to learn about relationships and how they work. Don't worry too much, this rarely carries forward to adult life.

I hope you have enjoyed this final chapter. It was a bit of fun and I think it has given you some food for thought and some strategies that you can apply in your own home. So now all you have to do is to tame your teenager and to rid them of the alien within. After all, there is a human being in there somewhere!

More about *Help! My Teenager is an Alien*

Help! My Teenager is an Alien is not just a book, it is a whole new way of thinking and feeling. This concept supports you and helps you take a light-hearted approach to dealing with your teenagers in a way that empowers them, promotes understanding and ultimately puts you back in control of yourself, leading to a less stressful time with your teenage alien.

If you want to spread the Teenage Alien philosophy and be an agent for change around the world, then visit www.myteenageris analien.com

Here you'll find additional resources including free downloads, worksheets, tips and audio and video clips, as well as our global community.

You will also have the opportunity to further your journey by participating in:

The Teenage Help Centre

The centre is packed with information in written, spoken and visual form, dealing with every teenage parenting problem imaginable. We can offer you possible solutions, ideas and new perspectives instantly and, as the centre is so dynamic, we are constantly adding to it. Log on to www.myteenagerisanalien.com or email centre@ myteenagerisanalien.com

Teenage Alien SOS

A place where you get VIP access to Sarah and her coaches for e-support, as well as one-off calls or monthly call-in days, where you get to speak to a coach, one-to-one, about your specific problem. For more information, visit www.myteenagerisanalien.com or email sos@myteenagerisanalien.com

Teenage Alien Stories

Send us your personal stories about your teenage alien and how using the book has helped you turn your home life around. Each month, the best story will receive *free* membership to the Teenage Help Centre. For more information, please visit www.myteenager isanalien.com or email stories@myteenagerisanalien.com

Teenage Alien Help Series

Sarah is putting together an audio series that follows on from this book. This series will go into detailed how-to steps for the most common problems that Sarah deals with in her consultancy. This series will be available in CD form or audio download for MP3 players. For more details, please visit www.myteenagerisan alien.com or email series@myteenagerisanalien.com

Teenage Alien Workshops

Sarah and her coaches run occasional workshops around the UK on this concept. For more details, please visit www.myteenager isanalien.com or email workshops@myteenagerisanalien.com

Teenage Alien Coaching Programme

You can work with one of Sarah's trained coaches in a twelve-week programme around the teenage alien concept. For more details, visit www.myteenagerisanalien.com or email coaching@myteenager isanalien.com

Sarah and her team are also available for speaking engagements, consultations and customized workshops.

To find out more call 0870 751 8825 or email hello@myteenager isanalien.com

For more information on Sarah and her consultancy please visit www.sarahnewton.com

Recommended Reading

Renée Baron and Elizabeth Wagele, *The Enneagram Made Easy: discover the nine types of people*, HarperSanFrancisco 1994
I have about six enneagram books in my office but this is the one I share with parents and teenagers as it is fun and easy to understand.
Wayne Dwyer, anything by this man is worth reading.
He is my spiritual teacher and the person to whom I turn when the going gets tough.
Kate Figes, *The Terrible Teens,* Penguin 2002
I like this book, it is informative and well written.
Howard Garner, *Frames of Mind – the theory of multiple intelligences*, Basic Books 2004
This book is great, albeit very long. A great and easy one for teenagers to read is *You're Smarter Than You Think* by Thomas Armstrong.
William Glasser, *Choice Theory: a new psychology in personal freedom*, HarperCollins 1998
Reading this book is like going through the spin cycle on the washing machine – it really wrings you out! An amazing book,

though, and my philosophy is steeped in Choice Theory. You can read the easier version, called *Unhappy Teenagers: a way for parents and teachers to reach them.*

Diana Haskins, *Parent as Coach*, White Oak Publishing 2001

Diana has been my mentor now for nearly five years and I love her and the work she does so much. My journey started with me reading this book. Diana now has a worldwide business and trains coaches around the globe. See www.parentascoach academy.com for more information.

Michael Riera, *Uncommon Sense for Parents of Teenagers*, Celestial Arts 1995

This is a great book that discusses natural consequences in an easy-to-understand way.

Jeremy Roche and Stanley Tucker, *Youth in Society*, Sage Publications, The Open University 1997

I had to read this book as part of a course. This is where I stumbled upon the Conditions of Adulthood idea.

Robin Sharma, *Family Wisdom from the Monk who Sold his Ferrari: nurturing the leader within your child*, Hay House Inc 2003

I love Robin Sharma and this book. His style of writing is easy to read and you learn loads.

Barbara Strauch, *Why are they so weird?*, Bloomsbury 2003

I love this book and read it in a weekend. It makes you go, 'Ah! Now I see ...' It is quite scientific, however, so if you want an easier version, try *Blame My Brain* by Nicola Morgan.